WHAT'S
AHEAD
FOR THE
CHURCHES?

WHAT'S AHEAD FOR THE CHURCHES?

A Report from
THE CHRISTIAN
CENTURY

edited by
Kyle Haselden and
Martin E. Marty

SHEED AND WARD : New York

© Sheed & Ward, Inc., 1964

© The Christian Century, 1963

Library of Congress Catalog Card Number 64-20407

Manufactured in the United States of America

CONTENTS

40573

WHAT'S AHEAD FOR THE CHURCHES?

INTRODUCTION

Kyle Haselden

Behind the 1963 series of *Christian Century* articles which produced this book there occurred in the same journal an earlier,
1961-62, series which described the background against which
there later arose the question, "What's ahead for the churches?"
A glance at that background prepares us for the opinions which
in this present volume forecast the future of the churches.

In the 1961-62 series, "Battlelines of Christendom," the editors
of *The Christian Century* sought descriptions of the enemies
threatening the churches. It can be taken for granted that the
20th century churches are under massive assault. For the first time
in history the growth of the world's population is outstripping
the growth of the church. For the first time in history Christianity
is up against formidable foes, spiritual and/or physical, in every
corner of the globe. The nature of the conflict and of the threat
to Christendom varies from country to country and from region
to region. It is one kind of peril in North Africa and another kind
in South Africa; the threat in Japan differs from the threat in
France or Spain. But whatever the variations, the danger is real and
must be faced up to. Are Christians "being closed in upon for the
last time" in Europe? Are missionaries being thrown out along
with Colonialism? Does the communist advance spell the doom of
the church? Is religiously prosperous America falling for a new
paganism?

To answer these questions *The Christian Century* asked a discerning crew of writers to report on the great battle for the soul

of the world from the parts of the globe they knew best. The answers were no less disturbing than the questions. As the reports came in from various areas of the world evidence piled up that Christendom, if not Christianity itself, is everywhere in jeopardy. Far from being a morbid sufferer from delusions of persecution the church reels today under massive and crafty blows from multiple enemies: racism in South Africa and the United States; stagnant traditionalism in Great Britain and the Soviet Union; resurgent nationalism in Central Africa and Southeast Asia; vigorous competition from Islam, communism and various national religions throughout the eastern hemisphere; insularity and hedonism in Australia. Explicitly or implicitly, each of the writers in the "Battlelines of Christendom" series identified acculturation, the absorption of cult by culture, as one of the formidable foes of 20th century Christianity in his part of the world. This ancient and universal enemy of Christianity—what an editor of *The Christian Century* thirty years ago called "amorphous religiosity" —has also been thoroughly identified in recent years as the most subtle, pervasive and virulent threat to religion in the United States and has been condemned under a variety of names: syncretism, eclecticism, tribalism, nativism, religion-in-general.

The accurate identification and sharp condemnation of the fashionable, conventional, patriotic folk faith which today displaces pristine Christianity and Judaism as the nation's religion have not halted the reshaping of faith and morals into forms which fit snugly into the molds society provides for them. The enemy has been unmasked. We see it smoothing the rough edges of radical faith, trimming off Judeo-Christianity's offensive and difficult imperatives, tempering religion's rebuke of private and collective pride, substituting for vigorous doctrine and demanding discipline easily and universally acceptable conventions. The result is a people's religion, a consensus which tints all areas of the common life with the same pastels of patriotic lore and prudential counsel but which omits the light and shadow of pleasure and sacrifice, ecstasy and pain, duty and discipline. The enemy of *all* American religions is *the* American religion. That enemy has been identified and condemned; it has not been challenged by the churches.

About twenty years ago *The Christian Century* featured several articles under the general heading, "What's Bothering the Churches?" That question may have been pertinent then, but it is so no longer. It is not enough to ask what is troubling the churches when we know quite well that what paralyzes and threatens the churches is their complacent surrender to the claims of that culture in which they are immersed. The untroubled external security and affluence of American churches are deceptive reassurances that all is well with the churches. Yet the American churches' judging, revolutionizing, re-creating powers have been rendered impotent by a social order which has adapted and tamed the churches and which pays them abundantly for their uncomplaining conformity.

Against such a background—the churches everywhere in peril and nonetheless endangered where they appear strongest and most secure—the editors of *The Christian Century* raised in its 1963 series the question, "What's Ahead for the Churches?" For analysis of the current situation and predictions for the future we turned in this case to churchmen who would write from a denominational rather than a geographical point of view. We permitted each writer to describe the obstacles and opportunities faced by his own denomination but not those of another, expecting him in each case to be loyal to his own division of the faith but as critical as he felt he needed to be. In each instance the writer was selected because of his known concern for the church, his analytical talents, his reputation as a scholar and his acceptability in his own church family. That the painful judgments of some of the writers in this series would offend some members of their own denomination was to be expected. Within any church there are two or more schools of thought as to the liabilities, assets and potentialities of that particular church as well as a variety of views about the way that church should fulfill its destiny. Within the compass allowed him none of the writers could represent all the opinions or reflect all the hopes and fears current in his church.

In accepting the privilege of expressing his own opinions and interpreting the facts as he saw them each writer ran the risk of saying more or less than his fellow communicants would have him say. We are pleased to report that each writer took his critical and prophetic task seriously and that none of them used this opportunity to argue the superiority of his church over others. This restraint is remarkable evidence that the churches have not lost all of their self-critical vitality.

Any reader of this book who does not find his own church studied specifically in this series will be justified in asking why it was omitted. The obvious answer is that an attempt to study each of the numerous American churches in a series of monthly articles would have prolonged the enterprise through more than twenty years. Limitation and selection were necessary to keep the program within manageable bounds. The loose design adopted by the editors guaranteed the inclusion of the four major faiths: Protestantism, Roman Catholicism, Orthodoxy and Judaism. Even in this effort to be fair there was a built-in injustice, since Roman Catholicism—the largest and most influential single church in America—was granted no more space than each of several smaller and less influential Protestant denominations. On the other hand the inclusion of articles on Mormons, Pentecostalists and "Peace Churches" gave to these smaller groups a space disproportionate to their size and to their cultural and social impact on American life. Such disparities were unavoidable. It was assumed that each of the major Protestant divisions—Baptist, Methodist, Lutheran, Presbyterian, Episcopalian, United and Disciples of Christ—should be analyzed in separate studies. The variety of opinions produced by this plan proves the wisdom of this assumption.

As the series moved toward publication in book form two rectifiable deficiencies appeared. First, it was apparent that some of the studies of major churches deserved a fuller treatment. Several of the authors were therefore requested to extend in this volume the statements which they had made in their original articles. To the writers who complied with this request we express gratitude for their willingness to assume this additional assignment. Second, although the series in its original form raised and answered the question as to what is ahead for the churches individually, it made no prophecies about the collective future of the churches. By this distinction we mean something more than the individual churches' relationship to and involvement in the ecumenical movement. We need not only to explore the prospects of the separate churches, including their move toward unity, but also to project on the basis of their present condition a picture of their common destiny. To meet this need we have added to the original sixteen articles two chapters: one by Martin E. Marty, University of Chicago divinity school professor and associate editor of *The Christian Century*, on the interplay of church and culture and the other my own conjectures about the coming relationship of the churches to the social issues. Several of the original articles have been revised and expanded since their appearance in *The Christian Century*.

The editors express gratitude to The Christian Century Foundation for permission to republish these articles and to Sheed and Ward for its gracious cooperation in preparing this book. We are thankful also to the contributors who ventured with us into the unknown future in an attempt to see which way the churches are going. Everyone who participated in this project hopes that "What's Ahead for the Churches?" has accurately and helpfully marked the areas of danger and decay, challenge and opportunity, which await the churches in the years ahead.

THE FORMS AND THE FUTURE

Martin E. Marty*

All but three of those who write chapters in the main body of this book speak in the name of one or another of the Protestant denominations. The other three represent Eastern Orthodoxy, Roman Catholicism, and Judaism. Each of these is also regarded as a denomination in the public eye, but my remarks will be restricted to the Protestant picture. The editors used a comb with wide teeth to gather so much of Protestantism into so few clusters. Had they used a fine-toothed comb they could have turned up over 250 denominations. Some of the groups are small: "The Duck River (and Kindred) Associations of Baptists"; "Two-Seed-in-the-Spirit Predestinarian Baptists"; "Apostolic Overcoming Holy Church of God"—these and scores of other churches with colorful names help complete the picture of American denominationalism.

To many people in one or another of these separate churches, their own church represents the one true faith. All other churches are measured in distance from the truth represented by their own and all other churches are thus somehow seen to be deficient if not apostate. Other people in these separate churches make no special claim for the truth contained in their witness; it is to them one possible Christian expression, but others are licit. Still others in most denominations look toward the day when denominations may disappear into one great unified church. Meanwhile, those outside all these groups may hold a variety of attitudes. Some find

* Martin E. Marty is an Associate Editor of *The Christian Century*.

9

in competitive denominationalism the excuse to reject Christianity or at least to reject its institutions. Others have come to terms with denominationalism. They regard the form of church life inherited in America as having been somehow predestined by history. No one is doing much about the form, and no one could if he tried.

With such a bewildering variety of church bodies and such a wide range of attitudes toward them, it will be useful for us in this chapter to set the whole question of denominations and denominationalism into the whole picture of recent cultural history. Such an attempt to see denominationalism as a whole may help explain how the American situation arose, what is its present health, what are its prospects.

Christian faith is decisively shaped by forms which it assumes in culture. Such forms are inescapable. Those who draw upon the New Testament and the central Christian tradition concur: Christianity is not an individualistic faith for isolated persons. It may allow for Robinson Crusoes—people who are temporarily and artificially separated from the whole body of the human faithful. But it does not allow for Tarzans—people who come to their full Christian personhood by a self-civilizing process. Where two or three are gathered together in Christ's name, according to one word of the early church, he is there in their midst. These two or three people will make up a form, of sorts. When more people are gathered into the growing circle; when these people plan that their impulse be spread in space (across a world) and in time (into the next generation), the form will become more complicated. As it lives in an increasingly technical society, its forms will become more technical. At any rate, Christianity does not know a disincarnate, wholly non-formal response to God's call. All people who confess the faith do so therefore inside these forms. The forms may be good or bad. They may be able to be checked out in the light of Christian norms or they may not. None of this matters as we set out to remind ourselves of the main point: the Christian witness and spirit take form, and the form helps shape the witness and spirit.

Not only will the faith take forms in general, it will do so in particular. That is, a generation will inherit forms which are recognizable and widely accepted inside a culture. These forms tend to become widespread if not universal. Whether or not it would be desirable to invent wholly new forms in each epoch; whether or not it would be tolerable to have to "begin at the beginning" every decade, we know that raw invention is not possible because recognizable forms have been inherited and the mass of people will measure from them. But if these forms are particular and epochal, they will also have depended for their original charter on certain specific incidents or constellations of events. Some of these incidents will have happened early in the life of the Christian church; more often than not they will have occurred in the recent past when other cultural forms were coming into being.

If Christian cultural forms are based in events or epochs it must be further granted that when new events occur or when culture moves past an epoch all the forms may be called into question. Thus if certain phases or factors which occasioned denominations have been replaced or refuted, it would be uncreative not to explore what such change means for denominations. To call these forms into question does not mean that automatically they will be demolished. They may have been created to meet some permanent or highly durable human needs. On the other hand, because the events which occasioned them represented what was new in the culture of the recent past, the disappearance of the original occasion calls for historical inquiry and criticism. The historian or critic will not always make himself popular. Peter Abelard learned this centuries ago when he had to flee by night after mentioning to the monks in the Abbey of St. Denis that their abbey had not been founded, as was believed, by Dionysius the Areopagite. The monks thought that he would "take away the honor which was their greatest glory." People are often deprived of some security if the origin of their institutions is called into question or if the developing life of such institutions is scrutinized in the light of historical change.

I believe this thesis to be defensible: that ordinarily Christian people produce institutional forms in each century which are well-adapted to the needs and occasions of the previous century. (Obviously I am not referring to neat 100-year periods but to historical phases which approximate that length of time.) Mere cultural lag does not account for the fact that change is retarded for a century. More often than not change in the world around the churches is perceived but not acted upon. The forms themselves are easily absolutized and idolized, exempted from criticism or change because they are seen to justify man before God, to give him security.

Our generation seems to be perfecting the arts of culture-criticism without perfecting the arts which would bring about radical institutional change. The denomination, the parish, the mission, the pattern of education: each of these is called into question. All of the disciplines of religious study are employed to enlarge the criticism. The specialist in the Old Testament evokes the shattering word and power of the prophet who reminded the assembled worshippers that God despises "the noise of solemn assemblies." New Testament scholars try to recover the mandates and promises of the first Christian generation to use them as norms for later generations. Church historians ask that the developing life of Christian people be appraised in the light of ongoing Christian norms. Theologians ask whether the forms are congruent with the theological purposes of the church.

Those who think in pastoral terms wonder whether existing patterns best provide wholeness to Christ's holy people. Administrators try to discern whether vital religious energies are sapped by routine and trivial demands in a complex religious society. Educators, conscious of the many stimuli which surround children, inquire as to whether the clarity of Christian purpose can survive the complex of forms. Missionary thinkers question whether a view of human need on a worldwide scale can be sustained if

current forms provide illusions of self-contained meaning and
security. The social critic and sociologist has his work cut out
for him. One representative of these social critics, Peter Berger,
contends that sociological analysis produces more shock to
Christian innocence today than does assault on the historic faith
from Darwinist, Freudian, or biblical-critical corners. He may be
right.

When criticism of these forms occurs, defense will also arise.
Many motives can be seen in these defenses. Some people respond
unreflectively, not seeing that an assault on innocence may be
productive of Christian good. They see the critic as enemy of the
churches. Others will be more reflective. They will properly
subject the tools of the critics themselves to analysis, and there is
no reason to believe *a priori* that the critics work with a superior
wisdom which is inaccessible to the defenders. The defender will
normally claim either that the inherited forms are integral to
original Christianity or that they should not be changed because
they continue to meet the needs of many people. God is seen to
be working through these forms; it is uncertain how people will
respond to his call in forms that are being discussed or proposed
but which are not widely represented or tested. Such reflective
critics will be wary of unthinking propheticism and thoughtless
iconoclasm.

More often than not, defenders of the existing order, whether
they be reflective or not, will operate consciously or unconsciously
with models of "the good old days." Most Christians find something or other to have been ideal in the formative first Christian
century. Many of them, be they Orthodox, Roman Catholic, or
Protestant, will recall the decisive influence on form of the 4th
and 5th (creed-*form*ulating) ecumenical centuries. Roman Catholics regard the 12th and 13th centuries with special warmth.
Then Christianity and the surrounding culture seemed to be
related in an especially positive and productive way. The creativ-
ity of the relation is seen in the cathedrals or in the thought-
systems of St. Thomas Aquinas and others. Protestants tend to

place the 16th century (re-*form*ation) in a special location in their memory. Even more, I shall propose, the 19th century to many represents formally the climax of "the good old days" and is used for measurement of 20th century forms.

If the 19th century satisfies those who yearn for a past, we must ask why. To say that the generations of men often experience what might be called a cosmic nostalgia is not to solve the problem. Ever since Eden or Sodom men and women have looked back on the paradises or cities left behind. The glory that was Greece and the grandeur that was Rome call forth much in human memory. We look back to a Renaissance which looked back to the classical period. Those who admire the achievements of Christendom often try to reproduce elements of the Middle Ages. Most Americans conjure the memory of the age of their founding fathers to help produce solutions in times of insecurity. Men look back. The act of looking back needs to be studied by experts in the science of man and the religious impulse. Our only interest is in the question why Christians, at least of Protestant persuasion, like to look back on the 19th century. How can it be "the great century" to Protestant historian Kenneth Scott Latourette while at the some moment it may be to a representative philosopher like Martin Heidegger "the nineteenth, the darkest of centuries"?

The critics and the defenders, the critics represented on these pages and their attackers in *The Christian Century*'s "Letters to the Editor" column, seem to be facing off for a Cold War of interpretation. Both sides claim Christian and Protestant attention. Both sides in some measure or other no doubt deserve it. Why either side should be accused of bad motives we cannot determine: both may well have the desire to serve the best purposes in the life of the church. One might say that the present decade is an excellent time to go through a crisis of interpretation. In America religious institutions are sufficiently strong and secure to survive any kind of inquiry. Meanwhile in America non-religious impulses are sufficiently profound to call for religious inquiry. Our newly-recognized pluralism ("any number can play") has given a new legitimacy to every kind of social and religious group and has occasioned new curiosity. On the other hand, our newly-recognized need for national purpose and consensus has given a new urgency to every kind of unitive endeavor.

We shall on the following pages look at some of the needs which, in the period just before our own, helped produce modern denominations. What were the possibilities for the churches inside culture at a given moment? Then we shall look briefly at how the denominational form developed to meet these needs and in the context of these possibilities. Then: what happened to the culture and its needs and possibilities? What have these happenings done to change the basis of today's forms? What new possibilities are ahead?

Each of the spokesmen in this book was asked to comment specifically on a church body or a denomination. Most of them could have used similar tools of analysis and studied the local parish or some other institution. But the denomination and the parish certainly deserve priority over other institutions because in their modern form they tend to determine the others. Ask the typical religious American, "What are you?" and he will not need to answer "I am a Christian." Isn't almost everybody? No, he will say, "I am a Methodist" or "I am a member of St. Paul's Lutheran Church" or "I go to the Baptist church." The churchgoing and the nonchurchgoing alike recognize the power of the denomination and parish on billboards, in the mass media, and in thousands of public and private junctures in the culture.

The denomination, what is it? Here it is not necessary to detail, but only to refer to, sociological studies of the denomination. Most later studies still derive much of their definition from Ernst Troeltsch (1912) in his distinction between "the church type" and "the sect type" of religious group. The former was more inclusive and conserved the values of culture. The latter, or more exclusive, was more radical in rejecting many values of culture. (Troeltsch also foresaw the development of "the mysticism type" as the rejection of institutions.) Others have enlarged on

Troeltsch's definition, purifying the study of both church and sect and subdividing each. Thus J. Milton Yinger works through a set of concentrics from the most inclusive "universal church" through "*ecclesia*" into "class church," or "denomination," through the "established sect" and "the sect" to the most private and esoteric "cult." We should note that most groups like to think of themselves as churches and almost none of them like to be referred to as sects. Good manners as well as accuracy of definition should lead us to be chary of the use of the term sect.

The modern world, and particularly on the American scene, has called forth new terminology to meet the new needs, and "church" and "sect" alike have tended to be displaced by the neutral term "denomination." So dominating have this form and this term become that the foremost contemporary historian of American Christianity, Sidney E. Mead, can speak of denominationalism as *the* shape (form) of American Protestantism. His colleagues Winthrop Hudson, Robert Handy, Sidney Ahlstrom, and others who teach the subject today would tend to concur. Since "denomination" is basically a name for a class or group of things in dictionary terms, it satisfies the need for neutrality. In a sense it is an unsatisfying "nothing" word implying no substance and allowing for no value judgment. Thus it is so useful to the historian as he goes about his business just as it is to the American layman as he goes about his own.

When a neutral term enters history it collects a history. Denominationalism therefore does not remain a wholly neutral entity. Both those who inhabit the denominations and those who stand outside them find a new logic imposing itself on the experience of the term. Many people in the denominations would not accept or enjoy all the implications, but they cannot wholly escape them as described by Winthrop Hudson:

The basic contention of the denominational theory is that the true Church is not to be identified in any exclusive sense with any particular ecclesiastical institution. The outward forms of worship and organiza-

tion are, at best, differing attempts to give visible expression to that
larger life of the whole Church which embraces all Christians. Thus
no denomination claims to represent the whole Church of Christ, nor
does it regard all other Churches as false Churches. On the contrary,
all denominations expect to cooperate in freedom and mutual respect
with other denominations in discharging their common responsibilities
to God and the world.[1]

The denomination in a sense seeks to provide a neutral ground
which de-values competition, just as it inescapably advertises
variety and enhances competition. Thus a confusion of directives
("love thy neighbor; shove thy neighbor") is at the very heart
of American Christianity, giving it strength and life just as it
stigmatizes every claim to wholeness and unity in the church.

Sidney Mead has pointed to the "historylessness" of the denominations. Most of them are purposive, not confessional. That
is, they are organized in the light of certain community goals and
purposes and only incidentally as bearers of a distinctive confession. (A few are heavily oriented to confession of a creed, sometimes temporarily at the expense of community purpose. Mead
notes, however, that confessing churches in America tend to
advertise their confession as the legitimizing base of the denomination, and thus they, too, become "purposively" oriented.) A
historyless group, in a sense, looks less to the whole tradition of
the church and more at the specific occasions and purposes implied
in its own separate history. It tends to hop, skip, and jump over
Christian history to select the moments and witnesses which will
justify that separate history.

Since denominations in America are part of the voluntary pattern which grew up when the churches were disestablished and
church and state were separated, competition is implied. The
doctrine of the church is thus affected. In Christian definition the
church is the body of the faithful, not the sum of the faithful.
But as any observer notes, the latter appears to be the true state of
affairs. A denomination sends a representative (usually a cleric)

[1] *Crossroads*, VII, 29.

into a community. He gathers people around a purpose, or because they are of a like mind. They form a new congregation. They affiliate with the national group. They seem to be initiating the church and relating to the denomination. They do not seem to be an organic outgrowth of the one, holy, catholic and apostolic church. They become missionary, for in competitive religious America the non-evangelistic will only hold its place. In the midst of population growth, the place-holder dwindles, stagnates, and may die. "To get religion" is a phrase of American coinage, according to Henry Louis Mencken. He who "gets religion," or responds to evangelism, finds himself in one or another of the denominations.

If some of this is implied in the denominational pattern, it is possible to date with some accuracy the beginning and end of the cultural epoch which occasioned, gave plausibility to, and vivified denominationalism. To be overly dramatic, one might say that the era of the denomination was born June 12, 1776 and it ended in August of 1910. Of course, an artificial and almost phony historical precisionism is involved in this bracketing of the era. One must surmise—and hope—that no one woke on that June day of 1776 and said, "Let's give birth to a context in which a new form of the church will emerge." One will similarly surmise that few on a hot summer day of 1910 would have been thoroughly aware that what they were doing was directly undercutting the assumption of denominationalism.

In June of 1776, less than a month before the American colonials united to declare their independence, the Virginians issued a "Declaration of Rights" which is usually seen to stand at the head of a series of acts which led to separation of church and state where they had been united in an establishment. From that day in Virginia until 1833-34 in Massachusetts, supported by the First Amendment to the Federal Constitution, Americans worked out the details of a new relation between the civil society and religious institutions. Out of separation of church and state voluntaryism, competition, and denominationalism were born. Similarly the

Edinburgh (Scotland) World Missionary Conference of 1910 was
not the first nor the only evidence that Christians around the world
saw their mission frustrated and their self-definition obscured by
competitive denominationalism. But the meeting in that summer
was the most inclusive public symbol of the beginning of the
modern ecumenical movement. This movement has tried to call
into question the whole character of denominational forms. While
it has not begun to annihilate denominations (most ecumenical
councils are federative, and thus they guarantee the autonomy of
denominations) it has already symbolically ended the era when
the whole charter of denominationalism could still be reasonably
defended.

Before our symbolic date of 1776 most Protestants had accepted
the European solution from the Peace of Augsburg, 1555 (*cuius
regio eius religio*) in which the political ruler of an area determined the area's religious character and resolution. The new
experiment of religious freedom changed that in America. Now
the people who made up the political order of an area determined
their own private religious choice and resolution. After our
symbolic date of 1910 most Protestants began to give new assent
to those ancient doctrines about the unity of the church and set
out to see these doctrines embodied in practical church life. Some
did this by putting their energy into the merger of existing denominational subgroups. Divided Methodism, Presbyterianism,
Lutheranism began to put their own houses in order. Others
worked toward the establishment of national united churches,
as in Canada, the Philippines, and elsewhere. Still others considered
worldwide confessional assemblies such as world Reformed,
Lutheran, and Baptist conventions to be an excellent mode of pursuing unity. Most of them eventually were to find in the World
Council of Churches a federative symbol for uniting energies. It
makes no difference what form response took, nor does it make a
difference whether this or that group chose to "sit out" the whole
ecumenical venture. The assumptions behind earlier denominationalism were undercut.

The undercutting of the denominational assumption should mean the end of denominations and denominationalism. The charter for this form of church life, we suggested, was developed by social need at the end of the 18th century and early in the 19th. But of course denominations did not die and denominationalism still thrives. One might argue that since 1910 the separate churches have commanded even more loyalty and summoned even more energies than earlier. (At the height of the formative period of denominationalism in the 1820s through the 1840s a host of voluntary inter- or non-denominational associations were developed into great effectiveness. These served to propagate missions or to educate or reform America.) This phenomenon of new denominational energy substantiates our thesis: ordinarily Christian people produce institutional forms in each century which are well adapted to the needs and occasions of the previous century.

What was (and is?) the rationale for the denomination? Obviously it was not anticipated in the New Testament. Whoever makes out a case for his denomination as implied in the canon of sacred Scripture has to proceed not only on non-historical but even on anti-historical grounds. The picture of legitimate and justified competitive centers of Christian loyalty cannot be found in the book of the Acts of the Apostles or the New Testament letters. There even the first trace of merely personal (and thus sub-organizational) loyalty to anyone or anything other than Christ was confronted and purged as divisive if not idolatrous. The Middle Ages does not know denominationalism though it knows the churches of East and West, spatially and in some ways spiritually separated. It also temporarily allows (until the inquisitor swoops over the mountain top) for valleys of gathered sects such as the Waldensians, the Albigenses, or the Cathari. But Christians then do not work out of a practice or theory which legitimizes permanently divisive and somehow competitive witness and organization. As we noted before, the Reformers were quite uneasy with anything approaching modern denominationalism, and their epoch had no real room for it. A new environment, a new occasion was demanded. America and, by analogy or example, other areas where the churches were "younger" and where politics made room for pluralism produced the new and culturally creative solution.

What did denominationalism seek? Those who gave it its momentum knew that some form of church life was necessary to provide a way of expressing truth and faithfulness in witness. It is to the credit of denominational founding fathers that they took their witness and theology seriously. Second, they needed mobilizing and generating centers for the witness. The state church was disappearing. Governmental fiscal support and even suasive favor were being removed. What is everybody's job is nobody's job. So the churches worked to mobilize and organize loyalties along lines of distinctive belief in different areas and along the lines of different classes in society. Most of all, denominationalism was and remains a guarantee of choice and freedom. The offense or scandal of denominationalism was minimized, as we noted before, by a spectacular array of early interdenominational (and often laymen's) organizations of cooperation.

The denomination was an adaptation filled with genius for the genius of its own time. What is more, it met the American test: it worked. In a century when the church was meeting the new intellectual assaults of science and philosophy (Lyell, Darwin, Freud, Marx, Nietzsche, etc.) "the great century" of expansion came into being. There was always new territory, there were always new frontiers, there was always new space for a denomination to stake out its claim. Always, that is, until 1890, which is the symbolic date that so impressed historian Frederick Jackson Turner. Then, according to the Federal Census, the physical frontier was gone. From then on, in a sense, the denominations would, more than before, overlap each other's territories. They would, all of them, be competing in a sense for the heart and mind and loyalty of the same people in the same place. Each wanted a slice of the village pie. Edinburgh, 1910, was an impressive Christian recognition of the new offense of such worldwide competition and divisiveness.

If the closing of frontiers around the world after 1890 and the beginning of the ecumenical movement after 1910 changed the charter of denominationalism, it did not change everything. What was still "given"? Given was the continuing presence of numbers of Christian groups which had not yet found ways of fully expressing their Christian unities. Given was the continuing mission of the church even while it remained divided. Given was the continuing need for a relatively neutral term. On hand was "denomination," now entering an afterlife. Without being ready to buy all the implications of the simile, we are tempted to say that denominationalism now grew faster than the healthy ecumenical tissue—just as cancerous tissue grows faster than normal tissue.

If not all had changed in the 20th century, some things had changed. External expectation had changed. People were more mobile, more interactive, in greater contact with those who held to other value systems. Modern means of transportation and communication made possible the clash and confrontation of such value systems. Somewhere in this era Alfred North Whitehead was saying that just as Protestant doctrine no longer vivified, so Protestant division no longer awakened curiosity. One might say that right under the noses of formal clerical religion a new "laymen's religion" was developing. This religion was apathetically content with forms like denominations. To quote Yinger again: radical religious change was occurring under the symbols of non-change. People spoke in the terms of historic doctrines such as the Trinity, the Divinity of Christ, the authority of the Bible. But they made decision on other bases, and the culture as a whole was not marked by historic forms of Christian decision. The newer religion with its debilitating and relaxed relativism and religious universalism undercut the seriousness of the theology of denominationalism. The institutional form chartered to guarantee the seriousness of religious truth worked precisely against that seriousness.

A man can be confronted with 250 kinds of dessert in a cafeteria line and can rush home visually sated to enjoy the substantial-ity of a sandwich. People can be visually wearied in a store full of gewgaws, gimmicks, and gadgets only to go home and undertake a modest do-it-yourself project. And people can confront strident, competitive denominationalism after it has lost its charter and, wearied by the varieties of options, go home and figure out a private religion of their own. (Evidently some Roman Catholics must feel that the cafeteria line of Protestant denominationalism will lead the visually sated to the solid food of Roman Catholicism. At any rate, I have noticed that the appendices to Roman Catholic books on American religion seem to reproduce with especial delight the most extensive lists of fissiparous Protestant bodies. If I may be perversely Protestant for a moment, let me note that the joke is on the Catholic who prints the long lists: in American denominationalism the Roman Catholic church is also sociologically and popularly numbered among the denominations in the cafeteria line. Evidently good Pope John also recognized something of the same order—but was in a better position to do something about it. He saw to it that in the realm of public symbol and religious reality Roman Catholicism became a full participant in the *aggiornamento* of modern ecumenism!)

If the external or public expectation of denominationalism has changed in recent decades, so has much of the internal regard. Most Christians do not formally proselytize. That is, good Methodists do not go into good Baptist or good Catholic homes with the intent to uproot people from their church. Of course, some subtle and implicit proselytizing goes on, and ordinarily Christians are not unhappy to receive Christians from other groups! That is not important here. Here we need only note that in the denominations (recalling Winthrop Hudson above) an implicit affirmation that the church exists outside the enclosed denomination is made. More positively, many Christians who remain restlessly in the denominations are concerned participants in ecumenical organizations just as they share widespread human aspirations toward unity among men.

It may be folly to predict the future of the denomination. If it has actually grown, become stronger, gathered stronger loyalties in the 20th century after its 18th-19th century charters are gone (and without providing new ones), there is no reason to believe that the denomination will fade because it becomes increasingly implausible. It continues to serve as an efficient organizing center for personal and social integration in religion. It is a truism in ecumenical circles that denomination always comes first. That is, to take a fiscal symbol, ecumenical ventures are the last item to be added and the first to be subtracted "in a pinch" from most denominational and parochial budgets. To most Christians Episcopalianism or Presbyterianism or whatever it is that holds their loyalty remains a more vivid and demanding reality than the *Una Sancta*, the one holy catholic church hidden in the abstractions of its apostolicity. Yet an historical drift has occurred in the day when people around and inside the churches form a kind of "laymen's religion" which undercuts the witness of the separate denominations and perhaps of the whole creedal distinctiveness of Christianity.

If denominations and denominationalism do not wholly disappear they will, of course, continue to change and be transformed. They can be eroded into meaninglessness at the expense of the whole Christian witness and enterprise. Or self-critical, loyal, reflective, informed Christians can scrutinize them and assess the cultural role they play. They can re-explore the theological charter of the Christian church and ask how it may be best incarnated today—and then work to help incarnate it in living forms. None of the Christian authors in this book are arguing for a sociology of the church which is not theologically defensible and viable. That is, they will not be wholly dictated to by cultural need and planning. They will not propose merely "what works." As a matter of fact, this study is hard on the sensitivities of many members of denominations because it calls them potentially from what works to what is true. It calls them from mere accommodation to the practical and the effective, to the disciplined and informed life of sacrificial, self-giving Christianity.

Elsewhere (in *Church Unity and Church Mission*)[2] I have speculated a bit about what might be a creative future for denominations in the ecumenical era. Since I do not have new thoughts on the matter and since we are precisely on this topic, I hope it will not be taken amiss if I reproduce a bit of that argument. The denominations, implausible as much of their present experience is today, do serve potentially as incarnations of much that is good in the traditions of the church and of much that is vital in the confessions of the church. They are not necessarily going to be, or going to have to be, wholly dissipated or obliterated in a great vague globby ecumenical church of tomorrow. Their shadows and memories may well exist for centuries, no matter how ecumenism is spelled out and how well it succeeds. The question is: what theological basis will relate to these shadows and memories?

Take a cue from Father Gregory Baum, who speaks of the Roman Catholic church itself as "a family of apostolic churches." In his context the definition serves to justify Roman Catholic decentralization and to provide for a greater diversity in life and piety without a falling into anarchy. The post-denominational life of Protestant churches can serve similarly. They can be a check on ecumenical authoritarianism, should it ever emerge. (It now seems unlikely to, but one must prepare for contingencies!) On the other hand, these "families of apostolic churches" can serve as checks against anarchy. They can help gather sub-loyalties (as they now do without a clarified charter) to prevent the development of individualistic autonomy, or what Cardinal Leger has called "a purely charismatic society where each is free, whenever he wishes, to speak out . . . whatever comes to his mind."

The late Father Gustave Weigel provides a clue in a passage of mild criticism concerning Protestant denominationalism. Observing the half-hearted participation in ecumenism based on vigorous assent to its charter and vigorous participation in denominationalism based on half-hearted assent to its charter among Pro-

[2] Eerdmans, 1964, pp. 110ff.

testants, he predicted that the churches "will tend to become like religious orders in the Catholic Church—different modalities of life and worship implying no substantial difference, so that the member of one group could worship and communicate freely and legitimately in the services of the others." At the same time a closer union would develop at the cost of the conviction of many churches that their "creed, code, and cult are warranted by the truth of the gospel, while others are not." I have argued that that later cost has already been paid but the joys of the purchased product are not being realized in the post-denominational and semi-ecumenical era.

Jean Canu, in his study of the history of such Catholic religious orders, noted that they began as two separate ways of going to God (a Protestant would read: of responding to God). These ways developed from conflict to rivalry, from rivalry to emulation, from emulation to reciprocal interaction. This change facilitated mutual understanding and the development of a more complete and harmonious life. Has not this happened in Protestant denominationalism? Even the secular pressures of a technical society have imposed common ways of doing things on the group. In a bureaucratic society the various polities: episcopal, presbyterian, congregational, tend to function similarly. In an ideological world the common Christian witness seems to emerge in a clearer outline over against its alternatives and rivals. It remains for the church to recognize these changes, to incarnate them, to prepare for the future in which these changes can be enjoyed.

Now look at the separate essays in this book. Many of the authors would agree with many of the assumptions of this chapter, though I imagine (and hope) that none of them would put matters precisely the same way. What do they share? They are, admittedly in different degrees but still unanimously, loyal and committed to the "modality" or "order" which they represent. Yet each of them is critical of it and restless with it. Each of them sees the times to be out of joint for his group. Each church has a future, but that future is obscured because of present problems and misreadings of the past.

The writers were chosen for their general competence in their own disciplines, but in every instance they were to be either critically loyal to or loyally critical of their own representative in "the family of apostolic churches" which make up the whole Christian household in our time. Readers will be amazed by the numbers of places where the criticisms of one essayist agree with those of others and sometimes a bit amused when what seems to an author to be a private problem in reality is shared by the representatives of other privacies. About half of the writers come from churches whose history places them in a sort of mainstream of American religion. These worry lest there continue a process of erosion which broadens the stream so much that banks disappear and the stream dries. About half of them come from churches whose history places them outside the mainstream. These worry lest the happy moment when their groups enter the mainstream be marred by a dissipation of obvious values which were nurtured when the groups were withdrawn. Both kinds are highly aware of the creative and beguiling factors in the American environment. They all take the surrounding culture seriously just as they take their theology seriously.

I am not sure that many of them would succeed in converting newcomers to their churches by these essays. That is not their purpose here; they are not writing proselytizing tracts for the short range of experience. They are asking questions of the long pull. How do we set our houses in order or build new houses on good foundations, recognizable by passers-by as worthy settings in which they could serve the purposes of God? Haunted by the irrelevance of much in the cultural forms of their churches today, they are moved by the meaning and purpose which gave and could give life to their churches and to the church today and tomorrow.

1. THE SOUTHERN BAPTISTS

Samuel S. Hill, Jr.*

It is unlikely that any major religious group in America faces as critical an immediate future as the Southern Baptist Convention. Here is the nation's largest Protestant body, an institution with more than ten million members, justifiably proud of its statistical escalation from five million members in 1940 and seven million only fourteen years ago. More than this, the body has been incredibly influential in its region and accorded high status by the society around it. However, within the past three or four years it has begun to find itself seriously troubled within and ineffective without.

Until recently the Southern Baptists have lived as part of, not apart from, the southern world. On the active side, they have assumed progressive social responsibilities such as the support of colleges, hospitals, and homes for children and the aged. Moreover, many of them have been leaders in society, especially at the local level. In addition to their active contributions, they have insinuated their values, standards, and concerns into regional life at large. They have not had to be a conventicle people—as Baptists with their radical witness have been on occasion—for they have easily made their way in the South, partly because regional circumstances have enabled them to have their way and qualify as one of the most pervasive institutions there.

Little fault can be found with sociologist Wilbur Zelinsky's

* Southern Baptist Samuel S. Hill, Jr., is Associate Professor of Religion at the University of North Carolina.

suggestion that in the South the Baptist position was "apparently adopted as the creed most compatible with the genius of the region long after its personality had become clearly defined."[1] There has been a significant interrelation between Southern Baptists and the southern culture for over two centuries. The Baptist style of life has blended well with the regional personality—as a matter of fact it has gone far toward conditioning the outlook and attitudes of southern people. Historically, Baptists have been sect-type, radical in their isolation from or opposition to culture. Where Southern Baptists are found outside the South, they incline toward the sect-classification, though not so much for theological as for cultural reasons. In the denomination's homeland, however, they are church-type, running with the grain of the culture, being accepted by and involved in the culture there. For not only have they been accepted by regional society and influential in helping shape it, they have acquired popular recognition as the normative or established denomination of the region.

This felicitous relation is now being disrupted. Slowly but surely since the mid-1950's, social change has been effecting a milieu in which the Southern Baptist institution is gradually coming to be less at home. The New South, the post-Civil War context in which industrialization, urbanization, and improved levels of education began taking their place, now appears to be in process of gradual replacement by a new reality, the South as an essentially integrated part of America. The South gives evidence of returning to the mainstream of national life. The southern world is giving way to a different, larger world—and the people themselves are changing. The Southern Baptist outlook, spawned in and tied to a culture now passing away, is not highly intelligible and meaningful to an expanding segment of more cosmopolitan Southerners. The denomination's image in their eyes worsens steadily. Their rejection of the denomination is far more serious than the innocuous jokes

[1] Wilbur Zelinsky, "An Approach to the Religious Geography of the United States: Patterns of Church Membership in 1952," *Annals of the Association of American Geographers*, XI (June, 1961), 139-193.

which have always been passed at the expense of this colorful, provocative religious body. As a result, a relative decline in statistical progress has set in.

Meanwhile, all is not well within the Convention itself. Severe inner discord threatens unity. Reactionary groups gain in strength. Significant numbers of younger members defect each year. How this body can come to terms with the new culture and how it can hold that considerable percentage of younger members who regard the Southern Baptist outlook as an outdated vestige from a previous era are problematical questions. The gravity of the crisis is heightened by the paucity of leaders who are alert to the sociological factors at play. Even more serious is the short supply of thinkers who recognize the possibility of reformulating the changeless Christian message and their responsibility for such reformulation. Urgently needed is leadership which can discern the meaning of the objective Christian message in the light of current modes of thought and in the context of the contemporary situation.

Were the institution and its people less a part of southern society, the emergence of the new situation would create only superficial difficulties. But so integrally related are the Southern Baptist people to the regional culture that the advent of a new era in the life of the South threatens the equilibrium of the institution (which will adjust more slowly than the people themselves) and the relevance of its ministry. The upshot may be that the Southern Baptist witness will be confined to members of the upper lower class, and lower middle class, and to those persons who are unalterably oriented to the cultural traditions from the South's past.

Already there are signs that the Southern Baptist Convention is becoming a "class denomination." Non-Southerners may be surprised to learn that during the last half-century or more, one might expect to find a genuine class diversity within Southern Baptist churches. It is true that any given local church was likely to own a preponderance of members from only one or two levels of society. However, the denomination at large has included sizable samples of persons all the way from middle lower class to upper middle class, with the heaviest concentration midway along this spectrum. Now it appears that Baptists are losing their effectiveness at both ends, in failing to attract or keep persons comparatively low on the social scale and persons in the middle middle classes and above. There is irony here, for the same denomination which has criticized the Episcopalians and Presbyterians for being "class churches" is beginning to find itself a "class church," a denomination comprising persons from a specifiable range of society.

1

Many Southern Baptist leaders are aware that vexing problems abound. But few, it would seem, recognize either the crucial and persistent character or the true nature of those problems. So enamored of the denomination's success and its dramatic rise to power, wealth, and influence have the leaders become, that few can grasp the severity of the problems facing the body. Today it is fatally naive to suppose that the crisis will soon pass, that time will heal the wounds, that a more rigid enforcement of the old policies will answer the need, that stepped-up enthusiasm will combat the problems at hand. Southern Baptists have passed this way before, to be sure. This is by no means the first crisis the body has encountered. But there is a decisive difference in this situation. In earlier years, a patch-up job would do. Now a radically new understanding and approach are required by the new outlook of a growing number of southern people.

Seminary professors had been fired long before the birth of Ralph Elliott, the Old Testament professor dismissed on the charge of heresy by Midwestern Theological Seminary in October, 1962. But in those cases the grounds for dismissal did not become general issues. When C. H. Toy (later to become a distinguished linguist at Harvard) was asked to resign from the faculty of the Louisville seminary in 1879 because he had accepted the documentary hypothesis of Pentateuchal authorship, there was hardly a stir; Toy was so obviously "wrong" that his ouster provoked no serious demurrers. Critical biblical scholarship was simply not a live option for the constituents of the Convention in 1879. But times have changed, and in 1964 a steadily growing minority of pastors, seminarians and young laymen regard the critical approach to the Bible not only as a live option but as the only approach which conveys the legitimacy, meaning and power of the biblical message.

Two factors in particular contribute to the storm beginning to break with full fury upon the Southern Baptist Convention. The first is the rise of a new mentality among young Southerners. The different winds of thought now penetrating the Mason-Dixon screen have contributed to the development of that mentality, as has the provision of more and better education. Of great significance is the new freedom to be avowedly secular which numbers of Southerners in their twenties are experiencing. Whereas traditional Baptists vigorously withstand the incursions of biblical criticism and untraditional theological positions, a sizable number of young laymen react with a sense of emancipation when they hear the Word credibly presented.

It should be noted that while Elliott's dismissal was demanded and applauded by some Southern Baptists, it was lamented and scored by others. What is not yet widely recognized is that these two attitudes do exist in the same Baptist body and that both will continue to exist, with the liberal element becoming more and more a force to be reckoned with. In the past that element has been both sparse and unvocal. Today there is not only an increase in the quantity of liberals, but a new character within them. The old liberal was liberal in what he did not say (by way of attacking the petty sins and other religious groups and by way of stoking the fires of hell in his sermons) and in his benignly tolerant spirit. But today's young liberal is not passive. Unlike his predecessors, he is active and informed in advocating a greater theological and ethical concern. He is liberal in what he says and does. With the rise of the new mentality and the arrival of cosmopolitan currents of thought the place of liberalism has become real and strong, opening the way to a considerable clash. We may confidently predict that a growing number of Southerners will not be attracted to the church or conserved for the church by the old orthodoxy.

"Sacrifice of intellect," a problem small indeed in the old culture, is what acceptance of the old orthodoxy requires of ever larger segments of southern society. One may be sure that most of those for whom secularism is now an option will reject the church's message and ministry before they will assent to what they cannot believe with integrity. In short, the South can no longer live unaffected by biblical criticism or by secular challenges to the Christian faith. Many Baptists will align themselves with the new (for the South) approach, even if they must leave the Baptist denomination to do so.

II

The second factor, rendered even more forceful by the thrust of the first, is the trend toward greater centralization of power in the Convention's official agencies and boards, as against local or regional agencies and boards—an almost inevitable trend in view of the body's fantastic growth in size and wealth. Such centralization is a comparatively new fact of Southern Baptist life, for although the founding fathers envisioned what historian W. W. Barnes has called "truly a denominational convention, comprehending within its scope any phase of work . . . that the convention should desire to perform,"[2] the body fell short of that aim until well into the twentieth century. Borrowing a historical schema which John Cogley has used to describe the evolution of American Catholicism, we may note four stages in Southern Baptist history: (1) the period before 1920, the age of the country church when there was little centralization, wealth, and power,

[2] W. W. Barnes, *The Southern Baptist Convention*, 1845-1953 (Nashville, 1954), p. 32.

when the Southern Baptist Convention was essentially the aggregate of individual rural churches; (2) the period, 1920-1946, when the denomination was undergoing the process of institutionalization and was becoming aware of itself as a powerful force; (3) the golden era of 1946 to the early 1960's when statistics soared astronomically, property values multiplied fantastically, and the denomination developed a lively self-consciousness and self-confidence; and (4) the period recently inaugurated in which a bracing new set of difficulties will confront the Convention, the nature of which has, however, yet to be determined.

Skyrocketing expansion has produced an acute self-consciousness and a determination to maintain formal unity. The far-flung agencies would be all but wrecked were a rupture to occur. And schism would be regarded as unspeakable tragedy by hundreds of thousands of constituents who look upon the denomination's ministry as very near the New Testament pattern. In speeches across the "southland" one hears references to the Southern Baptists as the main—or even last—hope in God's redemptive program.

The fact is, however, that convention polity is altogether unsuited to a structure lately become enormous and complex. Unlike their northern Baptist brothers, Southern Baptists have in theory vested authority nowhere save in the local churches. Rule has been, as a consequence, "from the bottom up." This has had the practical effect of making it possible for any grass-roots movement—or in principle any local church or single leader, providing it or he could wield enough influence—to help shape or to upset the life of the entire Convention. In practice "the" Southern Baptist position on most issues has lain midway between center and right, for that is where the balance of power has located the position. However, recently arrived on the scene are forces which may drive group consensus farther to the right. One of these is the reaction of the conservatives, principally in the Southwest, to the "modernism" of the seminary professors, resulting in the development of a new ultra-conservative power bloc. Another is the reaction to the levelling off of denominational growth rates on the part of many who attribute the recession to doctrinal and moral looseness, and who seek to combat it by calling for "a return to the fundamentals"—surely a conservative battle-cry not calculated to favor dealing with questions in the spirit of openness.

A third force is the infiltration into important denominational posts of persons whose attitudes are less tolerant and creative than those of many leaders of the past. Perhaps this can be symbolized in the statement that the geographical center of the Southern Baptist Convention, figuratively speaking, has moved from the headquarters city of Nashville two or three hundred miles toward the Southwest. An increasing number of agencies seem to have come under the control of more conservative men. Winds of influence are blowing mainly from west to east, whereas earlier the cross-currents seemed to be almost equally strong as they met at Nashville. The Convention's polity being as it is, wresting of control by the ultra-conservatives from the moderates is not impossible. For in this connection, the strong centralization of power in the boards and agencies only means that the will of the ultra-conservatives will be the most greatly honored, and will tend to become the dominant influence in a huge institution which still prefers relative uniformity to honest diversity. Denominational officials have generally followed the strategy of responding to the currents and pressures from the Convention, rather than exercising strong leadership by way of creating and refining popular positions.

Enhancing the likelihood of an ultraconservative takeover is a potential merger of the two most conservative of the Convention's four geographico-theological subdivisions. Religious climate grows more conservative as one moves westward from the "old south" (the upper Atlantic states) to the "deep south" (lower Atlantic states to Louisiana) to the "frontier states" (Kentucky, Tennessee, southern Illinois, Missouri) to the southwest. What appears to be forming is a coalition of the southwest and frontier groups. The southwest bloc, characterized by self-assurance and a big-business temper, provides the drive; the frontier bloc embraces "Land-markism," a theology which maintains that the only true church is the local Baptist church and that such a church stands in direct historical succession from Jesus Christ. Thus it is obvious that the character of a coalition party stemming from these two sources will be both exclusive and aggressive.

It remains to be seen to what extent the middle-of-the-road segment which has generally been in power in the Convention can retain its leadership position, and if it should remain at the helm, how it will respond to the pressures and ambitions of the ultra-conservatives. Whatever ensues, one may be sure that that segment's leaders (themselves conservative by mainline Protestant standards) will try to let the will of the people in the local churches—in practice, the will of the pastors—determine the future course they chart. One wonders *which* people and pastors will prevail—the southwest-landmark coalition, or the moderates scattered across convention territory who, though not liberal, do favor a free and progressive tone in denominational life. The conservative coalition has the better chance, if for no other reason than that it is more persuasive and emotionally effective. The liberals, few in number and largely concentrated in Virginia and North Carolina, cannot realistically be expected to win the day or even to influence the future course significantly. Yet one also wonders if circumstances and a widening circle of better understanding will not prompt the Southern Baptist people at large to acknowledge the inevitability and appropriateness of variety within the body. For the same reason that makes it difficult for an extremist to be elected to a high political office, the Convention may determine that its leadership and approach will never veer too far toward the right. To the present, the striving for a unity which borders on uniformity has characterized Convention attitudes. Perhaps the confrontation with an unprecedented cultural situation, and the cultivation of greater theological astuteness, will create a context in which diversity of opinion and approach will be welcomed as consistent with the Baptist outlook and salutary for the body as a whole.

The one realistic hope for preventing the transfer of Southern Baptist leadership to ultraconservative hands lies in the influence young ministers and laymen trained since the mid-1950's may be able to exert. Many liberated young minds are being turned out in some of the denominational colleges and seminaries, as well as in state and private colleges. As noted earlier, these persons are liberal in a different, more aggressive sense than the older generation of liberals. What they set their hands to will feel the impact, issuing quite possibly in a modification of the denomination's patterns of life and thought. If the conservative coming-to-power can be forestalled for fifteen to twenty years, a new breed may assume leadership. Dimming this hope is the strong pressure felt by the more liberal clergy, once in the pastorate, to return to the orthodox ranks. Now, however, there is more obvious reason for resisting the pressure. One matter which looms large at this point is whether young men of outstanding ability will enter the ministry of this denomination. Quantity has fallen off in recent years; perhaps quality will too. Furthermore, one knows of too many recent seminarians who have left the ministry outright, or who have turned from the pastoral vocation to the teaching field. Yet there is reason to hope that the Convention will be directed by capable men sensitive to the new realities of the contemporary situation.

The next two decades will be decisive. Unless the conservative blocs can be withstood, the Southern Baptist Convention will find itself in the hands of ultraconservative forces. If that were to happen, in time its outreach would be virtually restricted to the less well-educated and to authentic conservatives. In such a case, the denomination would be sect-type, cut off by its own design, as well as by its image, from ongoing national life. In one respect this prospect is not so serious, for after all a majority of southerners will continue to be fertile soil for the traditional Southern Baptist approach. But it is heartbreaking to contemplate the probability that this Christian body will have less and less and, finally, no effect on regional leaders at all levels in all areas of life. One is not cheered by the possible restriction of Baptist influence to the less well-educated and more provincial in a new society whose leadership will be educated and cosmopolitan.

III

At least four concrete courses of action will be necessary if Southern Baptists are to reverse the reactionary direction in which they are now moving and prepare themselves for a significant ministry to the new society.

First, they must acknowledge that authority is vested, that an authorityless institution is an impossibility, and that even if the shift represents a compromise with theory, the Convention simply must decide to place authority in the hands of perceptive, skilled, knowledgeable persons. Under present conditions, the leadership is wherever the strongest political movement in the Convention would have it be. There is a crying need for more creative leadership from persons entrusted with moving the body in directions in which their expertise advises them, without either kowtowing to pressure blocs or riding roughshod over the people and leaving them behind. Today, as noted above, any local church, any pastor, any group of churches and pastors can determine Convention policy. The whole denomination is now potentially at the mercy of men who are at best naive and untrained, at worst arrogant and demagogic. Traditional Baptist polity is not worth maintaining if this is the best it can do. Some form of modified democracy, akin to that by which our nation operates, is infinitely preferable to rule by lowest common denominator.

Southern Baptists need not violate Baptist tradition to effect such a change, since the early English Baptists accorded considerable power to the Association and contemporary American and British Baptists endow delegated commissions and boards with responsibility for decision-making. The Southern Baptist *modus vivendi* would be substantially improved if: (1) its institutions of higher learning could be controlled by boards made up of men familiar with the nature of education, and empowered to press ahead in the development of educational excellence, free from uninformed popular opinion; (2) it could set up and empower well-chosen commissions to decide on matters such as social issues and relations with other Baptist bodies; (3) its Christian education literature could be produced by skilled persons not only aware of the present level of the people and their traditional belief but also possessed of the most perceptive insights of theology; (4) it could replace with commitment to a progressive, comprehensive, enlightened ministry the present tendency to conform to tradition and to appease potential troublemakers.

Second, Southern Baptists need to undertake self-study, to practice self-criticism, most of all to achieve perspective on themselves. Ears have yet to be attuned to voices both inside and outside the family which call into question the Convention's beliefs and practices. At present an inherent defensiveness against criticism—or, more accurately, a kind ignoring of all criticism—prevails. Like all rapidly burgeoning institutions the Southern Baptist Convention, still *nouveau riche*, is somewhat insecure, loath to take a long look at itself. It would do well to use the period of relative numerical stability just commencing for examination and adjustment. Only so can it avoid having frustration added to frustration as the pace of its growth decreases and its influence weakens.

Several factors inhibit the free flow of self-examination and self-modification. Among them are certain regional characteristics—a nonreflective temper, a gentility of spirit, a disinclination to acknowledge the controversial or the undesirable. In addition, there is the pressure to be traditional in order to prevent the eruption of masses of pastors meagerly trained but militantly outspoken; always the leadership has to be on guard to keep in check the explosive untrained clergy. The Southern Baptist practice of making so little of ordination, resulting in their ordaining many men before they receive theological training, has played havoc with seminary education. For many, seminary education does not "take," through no particular fault of the seminaries. One goes to seminary in order to obtain his credentials and in order to learn to do more efficiently and effectually what he has already been doing. Too few seminarians throw themselves into the educational experience with the abandon required by the real nature of the experience. For this reason some of the functionally untrained clergy are in fact seminary graduates. Another restraining factor is unawareness that examination of other Christian positions and methods might prove exceedingly helpful. Finally, the overrating of the Southern Baptist access to divine truth and procedure and regarding statistics as the ultimate index of divine favor play a powerful part in blocking serious efforts at self-modification.

A third course of action is the one most needed. Southern Baptists have so far not seen the relevance of relevance. As one pastor recently put it, "All this talk about relevance has some of us southern churchmen confused." This is true because Southern Baptists have recognized only one responsibility—faithfulness to the literal Word as they interpret it. They have not seen that the Christian message has many sides and many possible interpretations; they have failed to realize that many citizens of the new society will simply have no reason to embrace that message until it is related to their lives in intelligible ways. For example, when the Christian message bypasses the great personal and social ills of our day to concentrate wholly or primarily on one's status before a judgmental God in the life to come, it sounds hollow and harsh. Many would prefer the hell of which they are warned to a life, now and beyond death, with a God who is made to appear less than fully concerned for persons in the here and now, and largely concerned for the restoration of his own offended dignity. Many have come to feel that a God, belief in whom is not comprehensive and emancipating and healing, is hardly worthy of the devotion of one's life.

Fourth, this enormous Protestant body must assume responsibility for resolving the region's (and the nation's) most pressing

social problem, the place of the Negro in the society.[3] Throughout much of their history, the Southern Baptists have manifested
concern for the Negroes, in bending efforts to bring about the
salvation of Negro souls. In so doing they have rather commend-
ably discharged their obligations to Negro friends and neighbors—
that is, in line with their definition of "soul" as that *part* of man
which lives on after death, hence must be readied for the presence
of the Almighty. Now a minority of leaders is coming to see
that the biblical meaning of soul is the whole man, that man is "a
living soul." As this awareness spreads, so will a deepening concern for ministering to and sharing life with Negro persons, no
longer in a framework of "separate but equal," nor even in a
framework of "equality," but in a relationship of brothers. By
undertaking a genuine ministry to this "other kind" of Southerners, the Southern Baptists would not only quash charges of hypoc-
risy, inconsistency, grave irresponsibility, and culture-captivity,
but they would realize the new spiritual health and depth which
accompanies the practice of authentic churchmanship. They simply must transcend the theory which makes the Christian ethic a
private matter for the individual conscience, and which concen-
trates on the retention of personal purity at the expense of sacrificial involvement in and service to the world. As yet performance
has not matched the denomination's official pronouncements relative to its Christian responsibilities in interracial affairs. Neither is
there any general conviction that this is a matter of fundamental
importance for the churches (whose central task is still seen to be
"saving souls"). At the same time, the denomination's Christian
Life Commission is providing daring leadership, and a healthy
proportion of the younger ministers is devoting itself to imple-
menting the will of God that justice, righteousness, and brotherhood prevail, and that the Christian fellowship be inclusive.

Southern Baptists do recognize the "there-ness," the given objec-
tivity of the Christian message, and they intend to be loyal to it.

[3] For a fuller statement see my article "Southern Protestantism and Racial
Integration," in the Summer, 1964, issue of *Religion in Life*.

They are comparatively free from the danger of lapsing into a naturalism or a humanism. Their belief in the transcendence of God and the authority of the Bible prevents this kind of heresy. (They do face the problems of oversimplifying Christian theology so that they are oriented toward inducing the single conversion experience far more than they are concerned with faithfully representing Christian truth.) This commitment to the quality of the Christian faith as "given" is one of the contributions they could make to the whole church if they were more closely allied with it. On the other hand, they need to see that their emphasis on particular facets of the Christian message stems partly from the fact that those facets were intelligible and relevant in the context of the frontier-rural Old South with its characteristic outlook, needs, and fears. That is, they must learn that their brand of Christianity is not the perfect restoration of primitive Christianity, that they have in fact adapted a certain received theological tradition to their culture. Reformulation of the message would not be a tampering with the eternal gospel—as they are likely to see it—but actually a step required by the nature of the gospel itself. And besides, such reformation has good Southern Baptist precedent.

At present the most educated guess would be that during the next two decades the Southern Baptists will be moving in a reactionary direction theologically, becoming more doctrinaire in temper. But what will happen once the new breed of laymen and pastors enters many key leadership positions defies prediction. The outlook and tone may change under the influence of progressive leadership; on the other hand, the liberal spirits, unable to remain and retain their integrity, may eventually affiliate with another Baptist body or another denomination.

Perhaps the Southern Baptist vocation in this age, so free to discard traditional outlooks in the interest of achieving relevance, is to "hold the line," to be firmly conservative or even reactionary. In such an age a reactionary agency can serve providentially. As I noted above, Southern Baptists might serve the universal church well by overemphasizing the objectivism, the givenness of the gospel at a time when relevance is claiming wide attention. But I cannot believe that a reactionary course is what the Lord of the church would enjoin the Southern Baptists to follow. At least in some of its concerns and emphases, the church of Jesus Christ must be out front, grappling with the lively issues and needs of the day, sailing the uncharted seas as well as securing the ship's anchorage lest it cut loose.

The Southern Baptists have come far from their simple beginnings in 1755 when the radical Separate Baptists from Connecticut migrated to North Carolina. Their life is more forward-looking, better organized, farther-reaching, less averse to cultural progress, less suspicious of education, and so on. Not all of this change has been good, however, for institutionalization has taken its toll of the genuine piety for which the body is famous. Yet, in history's long view, who can say that the Southern Baptists will not, in time, suit their ministry to the complexity of the new society and a better-educated population? The question that haunts us is whether they will be given enough time. The same question put more responsibly is whether this significant Christian body will re-orient itself soon enough to the new situation which is at present moving rapidly beyond it.

2. A THEOLOGY OF JEWISH EXISTENCE

Arthur A. Cohen*

No longer can the Jewish community be considered apart from the whole of the American religious community. It was once pos-

* Jewish theologian Arthur A. Cohen is religion editor for Holt, Rinehart and Winston, Inc.

sible to describe the evolution of American Judaism as an independent, rather ingrown enterprise. The American Jew's ancestral loyalties linked him more profoundly to the European diaspora than to the society around him. His history was European history; his faith was textured by European styles and habits (whether the rigid formality and bourgeois stolidity of German Reform or the peasant vitality and aristocratic manner of east European Orthodoxy); his longing centered on an unconsummated Zionism; and his theology was largely pragmatic, romantic and historicist. All that has disappeared. The European diaspora has all but vanished; the graftings from other lands have grown into a flourishing American Judaism; Zionism is now the State of Israel; and the theology of yesteryear is undergoing mutation in this new country of the dispersion.

I

The Jew is no longer meaningfully distinguishable from the non-Jew. His anxieties are those of his Gentile neighbors as well. Mediocrity, boredom and *embourgeoisement* are a communicable blight. The "ghetto" has become a popular category of Catholic and Protestant sociology, and "ecumenicity" and "Catholic" are finding their way into Jewish religious conversation. And both communities, Christian and Jewish, are finding it increasingly difficult to live above ground in America's suburbia or "urbia," and indeed to survive there with honesty and authentic passion while awaiting their true or false messiahs. One looks back uncomprehendingly but with unavoidable nostalgia to the days of the catacombs, when our forefathers at least knew what they were doing underground.

The Jewish community is coming to terms with the fact that it has been Americanized for nearly a generation, that it has won security and ease in this new Zion, and that, in spite of its pleasure at this condition, it has surrendered something indescribably precious in achieving it. The Jew—leaving aside that bleak and un-

fathomable creature the "Jewish intellectual"—no longer understands what his millennial election, alienation and exile entail.
Once he knew it in his own flesh, in the taste of his "bread of
affliction"; but now that history ceases to remind him he forgets
(like most human beings) what it is that he is asked "to do and to
hear." The simple fact is that Jews have become too trusting, too
confident of history, particularly of American history. To be sure,
there is always in their midst that wraith of the past, the survivor
of the concentration camp, to witness that history was once—and
not so long ago—merciless and cruel; but then they can always
yield to the historicist temptation to hypostasize their own American history, to hold up the image of America to Europe and to
hug the security they have found on this side of the seas that
separate them from the graveyards of their past. The Jewish community is becoming American in the best American way, by
glorying in a history still so short as to be experimental, while forgetting that it should learn again and again from a history so long
as to be providential.

But there are hopeful signs. At the same time that the ideologies
which dominated American Judaism in the '30s and '40s wane
—for we note the passing of identification of Zionism and Jewish
survival, and the decline of the movement for reformation of the
synagogue in the image of American Protestantism—new forces
emerge. Though it still enjoys considerable *ad hoc* power, the
old-guard rabbinate which by and large dominated Jewish Reform
and Conservative synagogues is losing out. The rabbi who preaches
the good news of the daily newspaper and the best-seller list or
offers his people distilled Freudianism is finding them more restive,
for they have caught up with him. Fewer and fewer young men
and women need the knowledgeable seminarian to interpret the
day's events and fashions. The theologically centered rabbi is
in a much stronger position to speak to today's better-educated
congregations than is the rabbi who is still trying to explain to
himself and to his people why he cherishes his folk atavisms. The
older generation of rabbis, those once or twice removed from

European Orthodox parents, remade their Judaism rather more quickly and willingly than did their congregations, for many of these men had enormous familiarity with the tradition and a passionate desire, equally compounded of love and guilt, to preserve in this new environment something that might honor the lives and struggles of their parents. Many of those older rabbis are to be reverenced, for they did preserve a Judaism in America; but they paid an often severe price.

I have occasionally mused that one of the strengths of Roman Catholicism is that a priest can offer the mass in an empty church. That Protestantism and Judaism have no such absolutely valid ritual tends to make every failing minister or rabbi something of a huckster and promoter, for in his desperation to serve and please (service and pleasure being measured by filled pews) he bends over backwards to be contemporary, relevant to the times, up to date. The fact of the matter is, however, that the rabbi—or the minister—is not really expected to do or be any of these. He has only to speak the Word of God, and, if the sanctuary is empty, to pray for those who had not comprehended how important it was that they be present. Many of the older rabbis did not understand this simple duty, for they saw themselves as defenders and transmitters of an ethos, as Americanizers, as men obligated to shape the conscience of their people. And that generation of rabbis carried out all these functions beautifully. In the '30s and '40s no other religious community in America gave to the cause of social justice as perfect a witness as did the Jewish community. The rabbis did their work well, and they had a rich body of literature from which to draw their proof texts.

II

The '30s and '40s are now but ill remembered; even the '50s, during which the world passed into the atomic age with a vengeance, are over; and the '60s, settled into an unrelenting cold war and a precarious peace, look almost familiarly toward the abyss near at hand. This is a new time, one in which the wings of the apocalypse can be heard beating. And in this time something new is beginning in American Judaism: a new theological intellection, a revived awareness of Jewish liturgy, a renascent concern for the relationship between religion and culture, a new tenderness and affection, not for Christendom, but for Christians who are indeed Christians.

The renewal of Jewish theology, taking its cue from those disciples and students of Franz Rosenzweig, Leo Baeck and Martin Buber who came in the '30s from nazi Germany to England and America, has become less of a novelty than an occasion for a fresh departure. Fortunately there are few "Buberians," "Rosenzweigians" or "Baeckians" in our midst, but there is no younger Jewish thinker of substance who has not been shaped by the ideas of these three men concerning the issues of Jewish existence. They addressed themselves not simply to theological questions as such, but to *Jewish* theological questions—the relation between "commandment" and "Law," the eternity and temporality of the Jewish way, the relation of Jew and Christian, the Messiah and the Kingship of God.

The renewal of theological existence within Judaism—the persistent and unyielding presentness of the Jew before God—cannot be achieved without a renewal of that distinctive modality of Jewish life, the observance of the Law. The movement to the right in present-day American Judaism is signaled not only by an increasing concern within the ranks of the Orthodox for a more profound understanding of the discipline of Halakah (as evidenced by the widespread Young Israel movement, the educational alliance Torah v' Mesorah, and the remarkable influence of the Lubavitcher Hasidim), but by such factors as the reintroduction in many Reform services of classic rabbinic formulations, increased use of Hebrew and greater emphasis on study of Jewish traditions. Within the American rabbinate there is a new and unembarrassed concern for the perennial significance of historic Judaism.

But, if it may be said that the rabbinate is "on the move," what may be said of Jewish laymen? Here the signs are less decisive, for they are less easily read. The Jewish laity has surely not caught up; if anything it is rather less significantly involved in the fulfillment of traditional obligations. On the other hand, it is perhaps more aware of theological issues. The older generation, although often lamentably ignorant, was still sufficiently tied to parental authority to keep the Sabbath and festivals, to worship, to observe the dietary laws. But though the present generation has broken with such "old time" religion, it is much more a "studying" generation. If one may judge by the large attendance at Jewish adult education programs, public lectures and lay institutes, it would seem that, for whatever reasons, today's laity is at least thinking seriously about Judaism before making up its mind. This is as it should be, for in Jewish tradition "the study of Torah is superior to all."

III

What is happening in American Judaism is encouraging. It is imprecise, unstructured, unchanneled, but movement there is. Moreover, it may be said with confidence that the movement is not secular in character but religious. The significant institutions of American Judaism—not the so-called "defense" organizations which receive the lion's share of press attention—are the national synagogue organizations. Though often shamefully parochial in their interests, these have but one major preoccupation—the religious education of American Jews. And while they insistently seek to strike a balance between American realities and obligations to the Jewish tradition, the latter would seem to be winning out. Such agencies make less of an effort than they once did to explain away the inconvenient, to dispatch via the glib formulas of our time aspects of Jewish observance which are palpably unmodern but which nonetheless partake of the divine. The fact that such institutions are moving more cautiously, are more chary than ever

before of ploughing up inherited traditions and values, reflects
not only a growing recognition that what is left is worth preserving, but also a realistic awareness that if more is discarded there
will be precious little left. Jewish religious leaders, then, are
beginning to acknowledge that in the past they often moved pre-
cipitously and irresponsibly to reform Judaism in deference to
American secularity.

IV

Lest it be imagined that this somewhat optimistic reading of
the condition of Jewish religion in America is the whole story,
I should add that my own attitude is one of deep-seated pessimism.
What I have described is not so much a renewal of Judaism as a
suspension of its once aggressively supported deterioration. There
is no longer any need to Americanize the Jew, to teach him
American ways and habits of mind by freeing him of the responsibility of preserving his older European (hence Jewish) styles of
conduct. The confusion of ethnicity and theology—an easy confusion in Judaism—has proved devastating. The Jew was rightly
encouraged to substitute English for Yiddish, to abandon European dress, to divest himself of those secondary and unproductive
customs and modes of behavior which set him off as a "foreigner."
But where does ethnic particularity in Jewish life end and providential particularity begin? Is there really, as some late 19th and
early 20th century polemicists argued, no distinction between
language and manners on the one hand, and the ordinances of
the Torah on the other? The view that there is no distinction—
together with the notion that all that depends on the ancient conviction that the Jewish people were elected and set apart is divisive
and anti-American—provided the negative ideology on which
was based the Americanization not only of that which was European in the Jew, but of that which was Jewish in him. The harvest
of this confusion is now complete. The situation cannot get worse;
it can only get better.

The renaissance of Judaism and the synagogue in America can only be theological. Such a claim will come as no surprise to Christians, but it is a sorely debated issue within Judaism. The antitheological bent of Jewish tradition is naive in its historicism. It continues to imagine that theology and Torah are in mortal combat, that theology is simply speculation—and idle speculation at that—which draws off human energy and passion that might better be spent in the study and service of the commandments. But theology which would yield such weeds and nettles would be false theology.

Theology is the enterprise by which a man seeks to understand his life in separation from and presentness before God. If it is his understanding of God's Word and teaching that he is to be obedient, he cannot but obey. If the way of obedience is the way of the commandments, he has no choice but to observe the commandments or run the risks of his disobedience. No man—not even a theologian—can pick and choose among the commandments. They are all the will of God, if indeed that will is expressed through Scripture and the tradition. But a man can—indeed he must—be faithful to conscience, even if it be a sinful and disobedient conscience. He cannot practice what he does not believe, even if his unbelief is the unbelief of pride or rebellion. But he can never—and this is where Reform Jewish theology is essentially wrong—excuse his disobedience by calling the Law obsolete, irrational or outmoded, or by confusing the commandments with preventive medicine, hygienics, or social and psychic therapy. There is disobedience in me and I confess it, not happily but truthfully, and I pray that God will countenance my disobedience and aid me through my unbelief. Such is the grace and mercy that I seek from God. But I have long since given up any thought of rationalizing my unbelief or explaining my belief. It is all the Word of God and my willingness or refusal to hear it.

V

Such are the rudiments of a theology of Jewish existence which goes beyond the prevailing ideologies of American Judaism. This theology cares nothing for the further reconstruction or reform of Judaism; it has nothing to do with the resuscitation within the American diaspora of the artifacts of an incapsulated Jewish national culture; it has nothing to do with Zionism; it has no interest in the sectarian splinterings of historical Judaism. This theology has to do only with the Bible and the tradition, the Word and the commandments. It cares for nothing else but these —to obey or to disobey them, but them alone. If one hears and attends to the Word and the commandments, something may grow and develop in Jewish life which is not mortal, which, indeed, has never been mortal. For what is immortal in Jewish life is the fact that when it returns to God, it is sustained only by him. And it is God's promise, which I am still prepared to believe in spite of the harrowing happenings of history, that is my assurance that such a people can never perish.

Jewish theology can never become the new ideology of Jewish existence, for by definition theology is for the interregnum, the period between the time when Jews covenanted to be holy and sought to be so, and the time when they shall once again seek to be holy and may become so. Between those times we can only stretch the fragile bridge of our intentions. But if, as I have suggested, our intentions are honestly to hear what it is that God has spoken and honestly to obey him according to his Word, the Jewish community shall have begun the renewal which will bring forth from theology the impetus for holy lives and which will make of holy acts the instrument—for which we now need theology—to apprehend and serve the living God.

3. THE UNITED CHURCH: IN SEARCH OF A SPECIAL CALLING

*Robert W. Spike**

To peer into the future of the United Church of Christ is to face a stranger bundle of hopes and fears than is the case with the other major American communions. We are a new body, but we do not know how new. More than twenty years of planning and arguing have brought us, just within the past year, to a major consolidation of the national programs of the Evangelical and Reformed Church and the Congregational Christian Churches. This consolidation has not yet been accomplished on the state and regional level in many parts of the United States. For many years we have been accustomed to thinking in tripartite fashion about nearly every aspect of the life of the church: *our* denominational heritage, *their* denominational heritage, *and* the United Church of Christ. And this three-way separation of thought—Congregationalist, E. & R., and United Church—was always conditioned by a fourth factor: the continuing Congregationalists, who for years have been interrelated with the activities of the other three groups while stoutly suing them in state and federal courts. Now "we" and "they" and "the others" are rapidly dropping away from at least the forefront of consciousness, and we are becoming more and more aware of the one label, the United Church of Christ.

* Robert W. Spike is general secretary for program on the staff of the United Church Board for Homeland Ministries, New York city.

I

"United Church" is still largely a neutral symbol as far as the future is concerned. The scars of the union are as yet related to the past. We of the uniting bodies discovered how wide are the chasms separating the various Reformation traditions as we sought to cross them in putting together the structure of a new church. From both sides the main drive toward union was the ecumenical spirit—the sense of guilt over division, the compulsion to make visible the fact that the mission of Christ in the world is more important than polity. This ecumenical spirit remains the major force, the center of intention, that makes the United Church cohere, that directs its future. Such an assertion does not constitute a homiletical whitewash of other, nontheological factors. The truth is that this spirit had to be the center and has to remain the center, for apart from it the United Church is hardly plausible.

As we moved from the agreed upon Basis of Union, through the lawsuits, on to the Uniting General Synod, and then to the writing and adopting of a church constitution, both sides suddenly began to discover deeper implications of their historic polities than they were previously aware of. There were misgivings about what was being given up, and there was determination to hold to these precious positions in the new church. The constitution was, in effect, a compromise document. And well drawn though it is, it provides few clues as to what the real stance of the church will be in the future.

Two anxieties began to emerge in the days of final debate over the United Church constitution. These anxieties do not reflect present fixed positions or parties; on the national level at least, there prevail a remarkable degree of harmony and a great desire to consolidate the union. But these anxieties do represent real positions, and the tension between them has to do with the significant difference between presbyterial and congregational polity.

In this case at least, the tension is not fundamentally between centralized authority and local autonomy. The Evangelical side of

the Evangelical and Reformed Church was notably congregational
in heritage, and the Reformed Church, though more presbyterial
in organization, participated in that general congregational orientation which in actual practice characterizes most of Protestantism.
On the other hand, many of the agencies of the Congregational
churches, particularly the home and overseas boards of missions,
were far more centralized administratively than were the comparable agencies of the Evangelical and Reformed Church. To
some extent the extreme autonomism of the continuing Congregationalists has been a reaction against this aspect of Congregational practice; the most bitter expressions of hostility from this
group have been directed against the leadership of the national
boards. The antimerger Congregationalists tend to misinterpret
the union as another step in already overextended centralism.

The real tension has instead been between those who cherish an
organic view of the church as a compact, integrated people and
those who cherish the tradition of functional responsiveness to the
needs of the world.

This insertion in no way implies that the Evangelical and Reformed peoples had no missionary spirit or that Congregationalists
were without a doctrine of the church. To a certain extent the
idea of union was congenial to so many in both wings of the
United Church because of the excesses of both emphases. "Our
German Reformed Zion," as John Williamson Nevin, one of the
great leaders of the 19th century Mercersburg movement, referred
to it, was strong because of its high doctrine of the church and
because it was small enough to foster deep familial ties and commonly accepted disciplines, but it tended also to be insulated
from the world and to be too dependent on common national
background for its unity. Congregationalism, closely linked to
early American thought patterns that produced much of the nation's public philosophy, in the past centry often was too open to
the various winds blowing across the secular society. It tended to
assimilate liberal gentilities too easily, too uncritically.

Evangelical and Reformed constituents have generally desired a broader church experience and larger encounter with the world; Congregational Christians have generally desired a deeper, more ordered churchmanship. But, in the process of union, many on both sides discovered how deeply they held and cherished the ethos of their own tradition. Close up, high churchmanship began to look like inflexibility and a too easy indentification of the General Synod with *the* church. Responsiveness to the times began to look like dilettantism and highhandedness on the part of the mission boards.

II

The two anxieties remain, but they are now in working harness and are no longer pulling against each other. The future of the United Church of Christ will be very largely affected by the degree to which these two spirits confront each other creatively and refuse to be smothered for the sake of a superficial harmony.

Indeed, the greatest danger that confronts the United Church is that it might settle for methodism in order to establish a middle ground between order and freedom. Such a compromise would displace what has thus far been the true source of our unity— the sense of a common ecumenical tradition, a tradition which has been developing outside all denominational camps.

The writers of the United Church's statement of faith were not bound by either the Heidelberg Catechism, the Evangelical Catechism, or the numerous covenantal statements of Congregationalism. The whole issue of the use of a particular creed or confession of faith was deemed subordinate to affirmation of the central beliefs of Christendom, phrased insofar as possible in terms meaningful for our day. The resulting formulation is an ecumenical statement, not a patchwork of history:

We believe in God, the Eternal Spirit, Father of our Lord
Jesus Christ and our Father, and to his deeds we testify:

He calls the worlds into being,
    creates man in his own image
    and sets before him the ways of life and death.

He seeks in holy love to save all people from aimlessness
    and sin.
He judges men and nations by his righteous will
    declared through prophets and apostles.

In Jesus Christ, the man of Nazareth, our crucified and
    risen Lord,
    he has come to us
    and shared our common lot,
    conquering sin and death
    and reconciling the world to himself.

He bestows upon us his Holy Spirit,
    creating and renewing the Church of Jesus Christ,
    binding in covenant faithful people of all ages,
        tongues, and races.

He calls us into his Church
    to accept the cost and joy of discipleship,
    to be his servants in the service of men,
    to proclaim the gospel to all the world
    and resist the powers of evil,
    to share in Christ's baptism and eat at his table, to
    join him in his passion and victory.

He promises to all who trust him
    forgiveness of sins and fullness of grace,
    courage in the struggle for justice and peace,
    his presence in trial and rejoicing,
    and eternal life in his kingdom which has no end.

Blessing and honor, glory and power be unto him. Amen.

Similarly, the special committee charged with preparation of
materials for confirmation training put aside the question of
whether the confirmation tradition of the Evangelical and Re-

formed Church and the nonuniform practices of Congregationalism regarding preparation for church membership could be amalgamated. Instead, the committee reflected on the best contemporary theological thinking about the nature of baptism and its meaning for confirmation, in the light of the actual experience of youth and adults. And the commission on worship has been informed by the growing consensus within all of Christendom about the shape of corporate Christian worship more than by the habitual practices of Evangelical and Reformed and Congregational Christian churches.

This openness to ecumenical sources has its hazards, however, in the very nature of today's ecumenical scene. There is great pressure to develop denominational consciousness. There are natural internal pressures within our body to flesh out and give meaning to what it means to belong to the United Church of Christ. We want programs and procedures that are tidy. Every organized body seeks some definition of its uniqueness, in its own calling. We do have our root traditions, but by the very nature of the union we have put them one step behind us.

But the pressures toward self-conscious denominationalism are not all internal; ironic though it may seem, the very nature of the ecumenical movement in this country encourages denominationalism, for here ecumenicity mainly means encounter between historic communions. The growing theological consensus is acknowledged, but it is not translated into its implications for polity. The size and power of the denomination still carries the day in interdenominational relationships, often behind a cloak of pseudo-theological sanctity intended to justify a particular polity.

III

Hence the United Church is greatly tempted to establish its own denominational image in order to play an effective role in interdenominational affairs. But if the church's strength is its ecumenical core, then it cannot fix on any position as being "historically" United Church or "traditionally" United Church. Other denominations have moved down this road before and found themselves bearing only brand names that presumed a broad ecumenical commitment, rather than functionally acting out the implications of that commitment.

The other temptation is to think that this dead-end street can be avoided by entering into another round of church unions. We have advertised ourselves as hoping to be known as a "uniting" as well as a "united" church—and this often sounds suspiciously like yet another claim to be the "bridge church" of Christendom. (How many such churches are there now?)

It may well be that other church unions would be a good thing, but it cannot be a set principle that any and all church unions are *ipso facto* desirable. The putting together of denominational machinery, especially when parts of it have sanctified odors in some communions, is not the first step toward realization of the oneness of Christ's church. In fact, it may be a step in the wrong direction if it tends to substitute structure for mission and to paralyze the freedom-and-order tension by giving too many hostages to harmonious relationships.

For this reason many in the United Church, while welcoming the Blake-Pike church-union proposal as an excellent opportunity to discuss a breakthrough in ecumenical action, do not see the proposal itself as an especially satisfactory answer to the problem of unity.

The crucial issue in reunion is the mutual recognition of the validity of one another's ministries (not just the problem of ministerial orders), and the decision to share a common mission to evangelize and serve the world. It is fundamentally a trust of one another's practices, as long as all are evaluated finally in the light of the gospel's claim upon the world.

Perhaps the greatest witness the United Church can make is to continue to insist that polity is fundamentally instrumental and to resist the temptation either to dig its own traditions too deeply or to engage in ecclesiastical horsetrading through endless unions.

What is breaking down the wall between Rome and Geneva is the growing awareness that the enemy is formidable indeed, and that the enemy is the same for both—namely, the pervasive doubt that either God or man has any power. The primary task of Protestantism is not to indulge in interesting but uncrucial self-education and fence-mending; rather, it is to begin to build new structures of mission in the world for the preaching of the Word of God where it will be heard. The United Church must focus on the missionary frontier of the whole church. To do so may not be a particularly strategic tactic for the short run, but we will make our chosen name a mockery if we do not.

The average member of the United Church of Christ may well ask, "What does this mean for me, for my local church?" Questions of strategy relate to the local scene more than is at first realized; at the same time strategic considerations are more influenced by the position local churches find themselves in vis-à-vis other Protestant churches than is at first apparent.

IV

If one looks at an overlay map of the various Protestant denominations in the United States, he finds that in every part of the country Methodism is the most representative denomination, while United Church membership distribution on the same map indicates how regional we still are, even after the merger. We have increased the bounds of that regionalism; Evangelical and Reformed Pennsylvania is added to Congregational Christian New England. In the heartland of the midwest we have added numbers to numbers. In nearly every other part of the nation our churches are widely scattered—and often lonely. There are those who feel that the United Church should be trying to extend its membership in a more even pattern across the country. We do have a responsibility to help in churching the rapidly growing parts of the country, such as Florida, the southwest and Texas.

Nonetheless, United Church strength will never lie in plenitude.

It ought to reside in extending the commitment of the church to its essential witness, not in trying to develop a United Church constituency in every community. We should search out the places for new ministries and new churches at both ends of the economic spectrum, and in between—places where Christ's church needs to be. We must make for ourselves a special calling that will not be a mere denominational promotion. This calling should be that not only of the United Church's national agencies but also of its conferences, associations, congregations. Perhaps the New Delhi statement on church unity could serve as a guide for formulating this special calling.

How can we of the United Church unite with other Christian bodies to do the primary task—witness to Christ with power in the same neighborhood, city, state and nation—without first moving toward organizational amalgamation? Can we devise a really instrumental polity of action and witness, with our eyes on the world rather than on committee structures? Such a concern would be enough to keep us all busy and to put at rest any anxious effort to justify our denominational existence.

4. AMERICAN BAPTISTS: TO BREAK THE BONDS OF CAPTIVITY

Howard Moody[*]

Born of British Protestant-Separatist dissent, nurtured as a minority sect in a nation having an established church, the particular people of God called Baptists today seem domesticated indeed when viewed against the background of their nonconformist

---

[*] Mr. Moody is pastor of Judson Memorial Church in New York city's Greenwich Village.

heritage, their radical and adventurous spirit on the hazardous frontier of early America. The American Baptists, whose self-identity came so largely out of a passionate concern for people, whether in the Allegheny mountains or in the jungles of Burma—and to a lesser extent out of the traumatic division in the ranks over the issue of slavery—appear to have accommodated themselves to the very society in which earlier Baptists were hunted and hounded for their heresies.

Just to recall the past of the American (formerly Northern) Baptist Convention is to participate in the paradox of our church's present situation and to realize that our development from a sect to a respected denomination has not been without its price.

1

Any effort to see where we American Baptists now are is almost sure to require the painful discipline of reflecting on the tumultuous years in which theological disputes tore asunder our congregations, our national boards and our denomination itself. In this phase of our struggle to establish our "selfhood" as a peculiar people, the 20th century collided with the 19th; the young firebrands who were exponents of the new revolutions in thought challenged the dry orthodoxies that had long stultified the church's thinking about its beliefs. In this altercation the fundamentalists, to their discredit, used statements of faith as clubs with which to clobber individuals and congregations they believed to be disloyal to the "true faith once and for all delivered." And to *their* discredit the denomination's liberal leaders quieted the dispute not by open discussion of differences but by political machinations. This strategy led to paralysis; for years the conservatives were suppressed, while the liberals were frequently stalemated through fear of disturbing the status quo. Every new program and crusade undertaken by the American Baptist Convention—from the Church Extension movement in the early '50s until the Jubilee Advance in the '60s—has been hampered by local churches distrustful of the leaders and by leaders fearful of the local churches.

Thus from one perspective we American Baptists are immobilized by an unresolved dilemma; our open wound, bandaged in the interest of what turned out to be a false unity, has yet to heal. Neither crusades nor reorganization nor fund drives have been able to conceal the breach, as evidenced in sectional rivalries between churches, in hostility toward convention leadership, in subtle and not so subtle sniping at programs and pronouncements, and in officials' resorting to phony secular criteria in evaluating the life of the denomination.

When not immobilized by the feuds and schisms of the past we American Baptists tend to be lured by the "sweet smell of success" down blind alleys of prodigious promotion and frenetic activity. Our state executive secretaries necessarily become religious hucksters who spend endless days and nights "on the road"—the Willy Lomans of denominational salesmanship. As a denomination we seem bent on selling ourselves in the open market of competitive Christendom; we feverishly search for the fresh format, the novel gimmick, the new approach which if packaged properly will lead to a new inpouring, perhaps of the Spirit, but, more important, of people into the churches. We Baptists are proud of our "God-given facilities"—e.g., our handsome headquarters at Valley Forge, Pennsylvania, and our beautiful assembly grounds at Green Lake, Wisconsin—but we are embarrassed by our lack of numerical growth. We have been closing churches faster than we build them, and we are uneasy about our failure to gain members in proportion to the gains of other denominations.

Notwithstanding our inner divisions and our wayward pursuit of false kinds of success, there have been some recent achievements that have given courage: for example, the theological renewal which began in 1952 with the help of the Board of Higher Education. And later the Baptist Jubilee Advance, which had been conceived of as another battering ram against the world, was by God's grace transformed into a theological testing ground where

Baptists could honestly face up to what evangelism might mean in the mid-20th century. The leadership of Jitsuo Morikawa and his able staff accounted for much of the genius of this movement. If not always precise in their thinking, the leaders of the Jubilee Advance at least manifested an uncautious commitment to God's mission as they saw it, and for their determination American Baptists should be grateful.

Though the crisis which our American Baptist denomination faces is perhaps the greatest in its history, we may not be able readily to grasp its import; this time there is no overt struggle which would test our sacrificial spirit. Nonetheless, acute crisis is upon us, and the frontier looms large once again.

II

In the past decade we Baptists have used—or rather misused—the word "frontier" in describing the new churches we have built (mostly in the green pastures of suburban Edens). Our "new frontier" has been the frontier of religious resurgence, of booming budgets and mounting memberships in areas untouched by the ecological laws of change and decay. Here I would like to use the word "frontier" to designate the locus at which the church genuinely encounters the world—and it is for certain a world we have never lived in before. How will our Baptist churches face up to that world? How will we throw off the irrelevant aspects of our past? In recent years most of the Protestant denominations have been engaged in a theological renaissance of true significance, but the task remains unfinished. It will be of no consequence to the people of God if the end-product of all our theologizing is a correct theology. If all that happens is that Niebuhr straightens out our anthropology or Barth corrects our Christology or Tillich baptizes our culture, then our churches will have been poorly served. It is imperative that the implications of the theological revolution be taken seriously so that radical changes in the forms and structures of congregational life and denominational organization can take place. We tend to welcome the recovery of theology so long as it does not threaten familiar patterns of churchly behavior. The theological revolution will be complete when it opens new ways for church and world to meet—and when the church becomes willing to live in and for the world, hearing its abuse, being reviled by it, and bearing its burdens. For the American Baptist Convention and no doubt for other branches of the church the movement into the wilderness of the frontier means making decisive resolutions about several areas of significant engagement with the world.

The American Baptist Convention is confronted, first of all, with the *integration* frontier. In many ways this is the most crucial test set before us. Indeed, integration not just of our churches but of *all* men into the mainstream of our society is America's most perilous and pervasive domestic problem. The typical pronouncements of ecclesiastics and church assemblies are innocuous enough, but local American Baptist churches do little to implement even these. We must be honest above all else: there are very few genuinely integrated congregations or church schools or institutions in the American Baptist Convention. Our Home Mission Society has issued a number of courageous statements on the race question; the time has come for them to be acted on. Right now a large number of Negro churches in Virginia are negotiating for incorporation into the A.B.C. Many of the leaders of these churches were trained in American Baptist institutions. The chips are down; the way is opening; it is now or never. What will be the outcome of our talks with Negro churches? Undoubtedly there are real obstacles to the acceptance of large groups of churches into the A.B.C., but these obstacles must be overcome. The walls must crumble; all the ghettos, whether racial or ethnic, must go. In this field of endeavor as in no other, we Baptists have an important contribution to make to American Christianity.

III

We Baptists have been so busy trying to become a denomination, so busy building architectural monuments to our "togetherness," that we may end up sharing but little in the true church which is the body of Christ, in which every wall of hostility is broken down and in which local churches are places where men worship the Lord on the basis of their common humanity. When we are able to spend as much money and expend as much energy on developing creative, integrated churches as we do on erecting headquarters and assembly grounds, then we will know that our denomination may have a future. Here is one frontier on which our people and our leadership must move. The countdown has already started in every large metropolitan center in the nation; the handwriting is on the wall, and its meaning is urgently clear.

It has been pointed out *ad nauseam* that ours is an urban nation; for a decade now "church sociologists" have poured into our ears endless statistics about that bloodless revolution. Ten years ago the American Baptist Convention sponsored a convocation dealing with our denomination's urban problem, i.e., the fact that our people are in the cities and our churches in the country. But like most such conferences it suffered from the paralysis of analysis.

The great problem stemming from increased urbanization, however, is not that we do not have churches where our people are or where the great masses are; rather, it is that the very folkways, activities and organizations of the church are irrelevant, sometimes actually anti-urban. Implicit in our attitude toward the city, even when we are trying to minister to it, is a combination of condescension and despair. The significant thing about the urban revolution is not that we are handicapped by inefficient deployment of buildings and congregations but that our whole way of being the church in the 20th century is shown to be inadequate, and for the first time we see ourselves as the diaspora of God—the minority that we truly are. Hans Hoekindijk seems to have had the American urban church in mind when he wrote: "Our concern must be then to make the small groups steadfast in diaspora, holding out against an overpowering environment which tries to squeeze everything into the same mold; with close-knit relationships which nevertheless remain open; an intense communion which yet does not make the group a ghetto, simultaneously completely dedicated and ready for service."

IV

How can the church continue to exist if self-preservation continues to be its chief concern? Self-preservation may be the first instinct of human nature, but it is not the first law of the body of Christ. If these new times require the church to take on new shapes and forms in the world—and it may be that in a world "come of age," a "religious building" will be an anachronism—what body of believers is better suited to lead the way than the nonconformist, anti-establishment people known as Baptists? The theology of the free church tradition together with the historical heritage of dissent offer the most potent combination for the initiation of a new reformation in Christendom. We don't need "presbyterial representationalism" or "episcopal order" or "Reform theology" in order to be the dynamic, relevant servant-people of God in today's culture. Our failure as American Baptists to be obedient to Christ in this new age is not due to paucity of polity or inefficiency of organization but to our captivity—not suburban or middle-class captivity but the kind Jeremiah was talking about when he said, "My eyes will weep bitterly and run down with tears because the Lord's flock has been taken captive." Israel was captive to pride; it thought it was much better than it was, much more faithful than it was, much more loyal and obedient to God than its life ever proved it to be. Our danger is that our captivity will prevent us from being truly free to revolutionize the church, prevent us from admitting that all the church's forms and organizations are expendable if they stand in the way of our showing God's love for all men. Everything is expendable save the operation of God's grace in the world and in the church, witnessing to what we, who cherish the safety of the "houses of Egypt," have forgotten.

The church always becomes a captive when it forgets its Lord. When we Baptists—and of course this holds true for other church bodies as well—become forgetful of him, we deify institutions, worship buildings, praise images and powers. But the only Lord of the church is a broken, crucified One who was freer hanging on his cross than is the church of today with all its independence and self-determination. He showed us how to break the bonds of captivity, but we are still trying to do it our way.

Will American Baptists be able to move beyond church-world dialogue to a church-world involvement in which they love the world—even as God does—enough to be thoroughly immersed in it and concerned enough to defy it, not because it is immoral or evil but so that it might become faithful to its true nature? Where is the church courageous enough to examine its own budget with a careful eye for the disparity between money spent on self-serving activities and that spent in behalf of the world? Where is the newly gathered Baptist congregation willing to forego constructing a church building and thus be homeless in the world as God was? Such questions are not cynical or rhetorical. The church must be willing to assume new shapes if it is to exist for others even as Christ was "the man for others."

There are those who claim that the American Baptist denomination has no future, that its distinctives have been blurred by ecclesiological progress. I am dubious about such prophecies, but of one thing I am sure: our future is in God's hands. The present, however, is ours, and if we choose the safety of the houses of Egypt over against the tents of the wilderness, we shall deserve whatever fate Christian history accords us.

5. THE PENTECOSTAL MOVEMENT: HOPES AND HAZARDS

Klaude Kendrick*

In recent years the Pentecostal sects have attained sufficient significance to be called by some a "third force." A development primarily out of the past half-century, the Pentecostal groups grew out of a wave of revivalism in which motor phenomena (especially glossolalia, or speaking in "unknown tongues") were a prominent feature. Initially this movement, which stressed perfection and holiness, appealed primarily to persons of low income who had become unchurched as a result, paradoxically, of America's post-Civil War prosperity. In this situation churches that had ministered to the poor were forced to attune themselves to the affairs, tastes and interests of the middle classes. Many of those who failed to benefit from the new prosperity became so uncomfortable in the established churches that they withdrew. It was among this group that Pentecostalism found acceptance.

I

The processes that are generally considered characteristic of sect development have been evident in the history of the Pentecostal movement. With a near-ascetic devotion to evangelistic and missionary enterprises, Pentecostal groups have been among the fastest-growing religious bodies in America, and some of them are now on the threshold of the "church" phase of development.

* Mr. Kendrick is president of Southwestern College (Assemblies of God) in Waxahachie, Texas.

Along with their numerical gains the Pentecostals have fared rather well economically. Their strict discipline and their avid thrift, aided during World War II by inflationary tendencies, have served to elevate them from marginal poverty to moderate affluence and to enable them to become interested in new religious, social and cultural opportunities.

The Pentecostal movement is now at a place where it must make a number of difficult decisions. Traditional values and practices are being weighed and appraised in light of new problems and conditions. The major part of all Pentecostal resources and services was once channeled into evangelistic activity; in terms of the movement's premillennialist views such overbalance seemed fully justified. In recent years, however, Pentecostal churches have lost quite a number of members, primarily as a consequence of inadequate programs, and many Pentecostals, looking for ways to minimize such losses, are now favorably disposed to programs they previously regarded as secular and contrary to New Testament practice.

In the past the Pentecostal movement has tended to look upon higher education with suspicion. Colleges and universities, so the argument went, harbor influences that could divert interest from Christ's kingdom and destroy faith in the Scriptures. The aftermath of World War II, however, brought a significant shift in attitude. A number of veterans who took advantage of the G.I. bill and went to college became devoted church leaders. Also, formal training more and more proved to be a prerequisite for decent employment in an increasingly complex, technological society. Pentecostal parents, now able to pay for their children's schooling, began to question their sect's traditional suspicion of education, and some began to support establishment of church-sponsored educational institutions.

It may be said, then, that the Pentecostal movement has come to recognize the necessity for a better balance of church programs to meet the needs of all persons for whom the church is responsible.

II

The foregoing brief analysis of Pentecostalism's past and present suggests that the movement will pursue a course of typical church development during the years just ahead; i.e., it will become more concerned with "institutionalization." Attention will be given especially to institutional services that will help avert further loss of membership. Foremost among these will be programs to foster the maturation-in-faith of new and young communicants—a goal which will require a broadening of the churches' educational functions.

Fortunately the Sunday school is already used to good advantage in Pentecostal churches, and it will continue to be a valuable training vehicle. One Pentecostal body has an active Sunday school enrollment more than twice its membership, and its registrants at annual conferences for Sunday school leaders number in the thousands. A worthy objective will be to match such excellent quantitative performance with comparable qualitative achievement. Pentecostal groups are becoming more and more aware of the fact that a one-hour-a-week Sunday school program, however effective, cannot by itself provide sufficient religious training. In time the Sunday school program will no doubt be correlated with local churches' youth, adult, and service training programs.

Now would be an opportune time for Pentecostal churches to institute uniform programs for children and for leadership training. Such a step would not be difficult in regard to children's work. Activities for youngsters have been directed locally for several years in larger Pentecostal churches. The years ahead should see this important activity programmed in such a way as to contribute to the over-all objectives of the various Pentecostal bodies.

Strangely enough, the Pentecostal groups are just beginning to experiment in leadership training programs. Such experimentation may well command considerable priority in the near future. Trained, volunteer lay leaders will be needed if the Pentecostal movement is to enjoy a period of sustained spiritual growth. This is another activity which should be closely integrated with the church's general training program.

III

The home, too, should be enlisted in study and devotional activities that would contribute to a well-balanced training program. Most Pentecostal churches have drawn heavily from rural areas. In the agricultural setting of the past the "family altar" type of devotional, in which the entire family participated, was quite common. The change to urban living has by and large made such a worship format impossible. If the home is to continue to bear its share of training responsibilities, the churches must devise an approach to family worship that would be feasible for our urban society.

Formal institutional training within Pentecostal ranks will also be greatly expanded in coming years. At present all Pentecostal candidates for the ministry receive their training in undergraduate Bible colleges. On the whole these schools have been quite successful in supplying the demand for Pentecostal clergymen. And the level of training has been high enough to meet the needs of local congregations. Most Pentecostal ministerial candidates will no doubt continue to pursue this kind of training. Special needs, however, are making graduate work in religion imperative. Bible college instructors have all obtained their formal training in schools operated by non-Pentecostal communions. Similarly, Pentecostals have had to go outside their own ranks to prepare for chaplaincies and other special ministries requiring graduate degrees. The larger Pentecostal bodies now feel they can delay no longer in setting up their own seminaries. If Pentecostal churches are to maintain distinctive characteristics and objectives, the students who will be tomorrow's church leaders must be trained within an environment that reflects Pentecostal traditions. One Pentecostal body has already voted to establish a seminary; others doubtlessly will follow.

There are also indications that Pentecostal groups will broaden their college offerings in general educational fields. Increasingly, Pentecostal youth desire a college education, and their parents, some of whom are still distrustful of higher education, feel that church-sponsored colleges are the best alternative. Since World War II several Pentecostal bodies have established junior colleges, and one has instituted two undergraduate colleges. Such educational facilities will have to be expanded even further to meet the increasing need.

Pentecostals must also continue to improve their physical facilities in order to consolidate gains. The frame tabernacle so characteristic of early Pentecostal architecture has begun to give way to more permanent structures. As this trend continues, educational needs—and aesthetic considerations as well—will no doubt receive greater attention.

Pentecostal theology holds that the "Pentecostal experience" is a requisite for Christian service. "But ye shall receive power, after that the Holy Ghost is come upon you: and you shall be witnesses unto me . . ." (Acts 1:8). World evangelism remains Pentecostals' chief mission, and the institutional developments suggested above should enable them to be more effective in achieving this objective.

Numerical advances and material improvements, however, are not the only benefits to be gained from such changes. An adequate, integrated training program will keep congregations informed about and concerned with their churches' high evangelical objective. Also, the new program will develop leadership and thus provide better-prepared personnel for directing and staffing evangelistic work.

But there are also possible dangers in such a program. As a church body multiplies its services and improves its physical facilities, the possibility of becoming engulfed in administrative detail looms large. In the opinion of many, increased interest in ecclesiological matters, together with a higher level of material prosperity, might easily result in a loss of enthusiasm for evangelism. Joseph E. Campbell, for example, in his *The Pentecostal Holiness Church, 1898-1948* issued a "solemn warning" that "danger [is] lying ahead.

Wealth and education are the two greatest enemies of the Church. The proper use of wealth and education is possible but highly improbable. These two factors have been the downfall of others before us and unless we take warning we will soon go the way of all others." And Carl Brumback in *Suddenly from Heaven: A History of the Assemblies of God* points out that abatement of religious fervor may be indicated by an "alarming decline in attendance in Sunday evening services across the land; or to the brevity of the after-meeting at the altar; or to the crowded condition of the church calendar which will not permit some assemblies to engage in revival campaigns; or to the ever-increasing emphasis upon the recreational aspects of the camp meetings; or to the expression 'our denomination,' which in these days is often on the lips of members."

But though dangers are implicit in the stage of institutional development at hand for the Pentecostal movement, it will, I believe, emerge stronger and more effective, having kept pace with the times in terms of program and methods but remaining the same in terms of doctrine and mission. By enlarging their services to meet people's pressing needs yet retaining their fervor, their distinctive characteristics, their mission, the Pentecostal groups will make a unique contribution to modern Christendom.

6. THE METHODISTS

Franklin H. Littell*

At the time of the Civil War, one out of five church members in the United States was a Methodist. No less a man than Abraham

* Franklin H. Littell is a professor at Chicago Theological Seminary and Methodist Official Observer at Vatican II (3d session).

Lincoln praised their contribution to the Union cause. They also provided a plurality of the chaplains in the Confederate forces. No other denomination had grown so rapidly during the first seventy-five years of the American republic, when—with the collapse of the colonial state churches—religion in America was shifting to the system of voluntary membership, attendance and support.

During the latter part of the 19th century the Methodists continued their rapid growth, from 1860 to 1900 leading all other denominations in the number of new congregations founded: 34,000. In both years, 1860 and 1900, they had the largest number of congregations of any denomination. During the first half of this century, however, the Methodists barely held even, while the Baptists have forged far in the lead. Although religious statistics are most uncertain data at best, the change has been dramatic enough to be worthy of note and reflection.[1] A similar slippage is evident in relation to the population statistics as a whole, and a recent study shows that at the present rate Methodism will be reduced to 5.16 per cent of the population by 1970.[2]

There are other, perhaps more important, evidences of the sensational decline of the Methodists, both in terms of public influence and in internal energy and discipline. The denomination has nearly a thousand fewer missionaries in the field than in 1923. It has fewer men entering the ministry than before World War I. And while the unification of the three major branches of the movement (Methodist Episcopal Church, Methodist Protestant Church, and Methodist Episcopal Church, South) was an organizational achievement, it has not augmented the power of the Methodists in home missions, foreign missions or social witness— three ready (and valid) tests of the spiritual energy of a movement.

[1] For the over-all picture see Edwin Scott Gaustad, *Historical Atlas of Religion in America* (New York and Evanston, Harper & Row, 1962), pp. 43-44, 160-61.

[2] The figures are presented and interpreted in Earl D. C. Brewer, "Bigger and Better?" *The Methodist Story*, VIII (1964), 5:3-6.

1

At the 1964 General Conference of the Methodist Church, action was taken to achieve union with the Evangelical United Brethren Church (758,000 members) and with the Methodist Church of Great Britain, said to number nearly a million. There was also provision made for continued negotiations with the three major Negro Methodist churches: the African Methodist Episcopal Church (1,250,000), the African Methodist Episcopal Church Zion (800,000), and the Christian Methodist Church (445,000). Added to the more than 10,000,000 on the rolls of the Methodist Church, such accessions would be impressive. But such unions, though reducing competition in some fields, are not necessarily proof of enhanced spiritual vigor. In fact, there is reason for arguing that the serious internal problems confronting Methodism are, if anything, caused by undue infatuation with statistical success at the cost of quality of performance.

Methodists have been affected, of course, by the same factors which have altered the place of all churches of British background on the American religious scene. After rapid growth during the 19th century, the Congregationalists and Disciples and Episcopalians and Presbyterians have also leveled off, or lost ground. With the development of the Catholic and Jewish communities, and with the growing importance of "late bloomers" among Protestant churches earlier isolated by foreign-language services (especially the Lutherans), the center of gravity in American religion has moved away from those churches which derived from British Christendom.

In early America, British Christianity was dominant. During the colonial period, eight of the colonies had state churches (Congregational or Anglican) and four of the remaining five had established religion. Until 1820, 85 per cent of the population stemmed from the British Isles, and the religious style of America reflected that origin as truly as the cultural or educational or political customs. At the time of independence, out of 3.8 millions

in the thirteen revolting colonies only c. 20,000 were Catholic
and c. 6,000 Jewish; the rest were officially Protestant. In fact, they
were nothing of the kind; for when the established churches were
terminated, the people left the rolls en masse. During the second
period of American church history, religious liberty and the voluntary principle obtained. Their work well launched during the
Great Awakening (Baptists and Methodists) and the Western
Revival (the Disciples or Christians), Protestants of English or
Scots origin still largely dominated the scene. Among the "revival
churches," having their chief growth as a result of the "new
methods" introduced to win the people back to the churches on
a voluntary basis, the Methodists were foremost. In the third
period, the age of "pluralism" or "dialogue" which we are just
entering, the earlier assumptions that America is a Protestant
country and Christianity part of the common law of the land
are no longer tenable. So far, no denomination has had more difficulty in accepting the changed situation than the Methodist.

All of the churches of the earlier periods of Protestant hege-
mony, whether of state church or Free Church background, are
confronted today by the need for radical readjustment of their
self-image and their understanding of their mission in a changed
America. For several reasons, the Methodists have to date shown
less adaptability than most others who shared the same background
history. The same factor which accounts for the decline of Methodist influence also explains the Methodist difficulty in meeting
other churches and confessions on a basis of equality and open discussion. For a dialogue to be successful, each party must listen;
but each must also bring his own contribution to the fraternal
table. The problem attending Methodist participation in inter-
religious dialogue, and the problem of the Methodist movement
itself, is that American Methodism has sacrificed the Wesleyan
norms which once gave the movement uniqueness and appeal and
impact.

Institutionally, the decline of Methodist influence began precisely at the point where—largely for the sake of making the

movement popular—the peculiar genius of Wesleyanism was sacrificed and buried. This same change of character, by which, to be sure, it gained the status of a social establishment in some places, also unfitted Methodism for a truly fruitful role in the dialogue with other churches and confessions.

The Wesleyan Heritage

The peculiar institutions which largely gave Methodism its integrity and flavor were (1) itinerancy, (2) lay preaching, and (3) the class meeting.

The *itinerancy* was used by John Wesley and the statesmen who followed him not only to widen the sweep of home missions but to protect the preachers: the gospel was to be preached without let or hindrance whether people wanted to hear it or not! In recent times the larger Methodist churches have come to operate on congregational principles in the selection of their preachers, while the smaller churches and outposts bear the burdens of an itinerancy system grown political rather than missionary. (Ironically, the voices most indignantly raised to argue that itinerancy still operates are usually those of persons who have never—or only long ago—been subject to it!) Now a system in which the original purpose has been lost, and in which the "choice" posts have been removed from its control, is not Methodist itinerancy.

As originally operative, a people who resisted the counsel and standards of the church would be confronted by a much tougher and more experienced disciplinarian the next time around. Today, the haunting apprehension of being moved in punishment for prophetic utterance, of being dropped into some nameless denominational pit for attempting to stand for (supposed) denominational standards, provides no mean pressure toward conformity and accommodation. As one Methodist bishop put it in reviewing *The Stained-Glass Jungle* (a barely disguised novelization of the politics of Mississippi Methodism), "whoever Gregory Wilson may be, he knows the Methodist Church." The persecution of the preachers in the two Mississippi Annual Conferences who tried to uphold the law of the land and the (supposed) *Discipline* of the Methodist Church on the race issue, and who found themselves without the support of their bishop, amply documents the point. With a strong and consecrated bishop, who takes seriously his vow to "maintain the form of sound words and doctrine," the preaching of a full gospel can be assured. With a weak bishop, many abuses creep in. The very quasi-military organization which once made the Methodists a significant division in the army of God now becomes a tool of iniquity. The fault is that the itinerant system is not maintained according to Wesleyan standards.

A segregationist layman gave utterance to the kind of pressure which can be applied if the itinerant system is abandoned—and incidentally stated succintly the Marxist view of the ministry's role—in an article some months ago:

If their advocacy from their pulpits (in which they are, in the last analysis, the paid guest speakers) becomes sufficiently obnoxious to their listeners to cause a substantial decline in attendance and gross receipts . . . the clergyman mustn't be too surprised when the church fathers arrange for his transfer to more favorable climes.[3]

This is the kind of thinking represented by various pressure groups of the Protestant underworld, such as the "Circuit Riders" and the "Laymen's League," and it has grown to the point of splitting congregations in some areas. The effort to suppress the liberty of preaching, to make the church serve unbaptized interests, is of course the chief wickedness. But the institutional fault is the neglect of Wesleyan principles of church order and administration. It is not hard to imagine what John Wesley would have done with such "false republicanism"!

Serious structural difficulties have developed in the more representative American system which mute preaching and gravely hinder the ministry. A recent doctoral dissertation on "The Meth-

[3] *The Emory University Alumnus,* XXXV (1959), 7:14f.

odist Church and Industrial Workers in the Southern Soft Coal Fields" revealed that in the areas studied (in eight states) three-fifths of the Methodist churches were owned by the company outright, with trustees appointed by the mine superintendent. In the churches the company paid approximately one-third of the budget directly, apart from additional personal subscriptions by officials. In the average case, c. 50 per cent of the church budget was met by use of the check-off system.[4] In the textile company towns it is not unusual for the preacher, unless he develops an unseemly sympathy for the union, to receive a regular monthly check from the company "under the table." This entire patronage system and control operates in defiance of *The Discipline*, as well as in denial of classical Wesleyan principles, and it goes far to explain why in some sections of the denomination "The Social Creed of the Churches"—of which Methodists were prime movers (1908)—is virtually unknown.

The general trend today is toward an episcopacy based on one Annual Conference. This has the virtue of being in line with ecumenical developments—"bishops in presbytery"—and also of bringing the bishop closer to the ministers and churches and their problems. Whether it will also produce more acculturation and accommodation is uncertain. A sign of hope is the fact that recently several bishops on the firing line on the race issue have let it be known that they intend to use their authority, which is considerable if they have moral courage, to protect their men from unbaptized pressures.

On the other hand, the cooling off of missionary concern and mobility has been accompanied by a general hardening of the arteries throughout the church. There has been a distinct rise of clericalism, with the bishops and the secretaries of boards and agencies the chief centers of power. No Protestant denomination in America has a more authoritarian structure. With the loss of direction and purpose, the very quasi-military pattern which made

[4] Robert M. Miller, *American Protestantism and Social Issues, 1919-1939* (Chapel Hill, University of North Carolina Press, 1958), pp. 208-9.

it most effective on the frontier has been used in some areas to suppress theological ferment, lay initiative and social witness.

The Methodists are still, some of them, so active in passing resolutions and making dramatic statements about social issues that the real situation may be obscured. The point can be made, however, by contrasting the actions of the General Convention of the United Church of Christ (Denver, 1963) and the General Assembly of the United Presbyterian Church (Des Moines, 1963) with the behavior of the General Conference of the Methodist Church (Pittsburgh, 1964). The United Church and the Presbyterians took binding action and appropriated substantial sums of money to implement racial integration. The Methodist conference was not half bad at the level of verbalization: brotherhood was affirmed and sin was condemned. But the deliberate defiance of Methodist standards by some congregations—such as Galloway Methodist Church at Jackson, Mississippi—was not dealt with. And the much-heralded solution to the Central Jurisdiction (segregated) turned out to be voluntary, with a major escape-hatch for those who don't want to face the issue of race as the "moment of truth" for the churches. An apparent verbal approval of civil rights demonstrations was carefully trimmed:

Even then, meticulous care must be taken to prevent proliferation of civil disobedience beyond most carefully prescribed limits.[5]

One delegate (white) from Atlanta was naive enough to take the floor in protest, but the solid bloc of segregationists kept still: having already worked out with the compromisers the hard realities of policy, non-binding, they did not really mind having a verbal sop thrown to "liberal" opinion (and bad conscience).

One of the leaders of German resistance to Nazism once said: "I learned just one thing in twelve years: the Christian should not verbalize a position which he is not prepared to make a matter of witness." This is a lesson which the Methodist Church has

[5] *The New York Times*, May 4, 1964; p. C25.

forgotten, as its standards of membership and discipline have collapsed. A chief symbol of that collapse has been the abandonment of the purpose and practice of an itinerant ministry.

Lay preaching was an office which made it possible for the itinerant to serve several posts, and sometimes large territories. During the time of mass evangelism, in the second period of American church history, lay initiative was prominent in the mission of Methodism. This is fundamentally different, of course, from the structure and intent of lay patronage. After a period of decline, lay training is being renewed in some places as part of the ecumenical emphasis on the apostolate of the laity. Some bishops have bitterly opposed this development and have reassigned young pastors who were encouraging their people in it. The bureaucracy still prefers laymen of the type most common before the Reformation emphasis on the general priesthood, before the rise of Wesleyanism: the type which is silent, docile, and obedient to authority.

Today, where lay training is cultivated, the stress is on discussion in small groups and on the teaching roll of the ministry, as well as on service to churches without a stated supply. One most remarkable renewal has occurred recently in the Columbia (S.C.) District, where, under the very able leadership connected with the Columbia Lay Academy, over 1,200 men have taken training as lay speakers. Their course ran eight weeks, they paid a solid matriculation fee, and they committed themselves to a sound discipline of study and service. Throughout the denomination as a whole, however, the men's program is still limited to popular and superficial social clubs, enlivened by an occasional promotional scheme.

The *class meeting* was once the key instrument for training applicants in the fundamental tenets of Methodism and for maintaining membership standards in the movement. It is still used to some extent in English, Welsh, German and Swiss Methodism, but in America such practices were largely abandoned at the turn of the century. In the 1908 General Conference of the Meth-

odist Episcopal Church the step was taken which the Methodist
Protestants and the M. E. Church, South, had earlier made. Until
then, no one could be recommended for full membership except
by "a leader with whom [he had] met at least six months in
class." This was deleted from *The Discipline*, and probationary
membership "under the care of proper leaders for six months on
trial" was eliminated. The provision that he should give "satisfactory assurances both of the correctness of his faith and of his
willingness to observe and keep the rules of the Church" was re-
tained, but there was no longer any structure to make it more
than a pious hope.[6] Significantly, the words "and thus far you
have run well" were also struck out! In Lent of 1960, in Atlanta,
a single Methodist congregation took in 462 individuals on one
Sunday morning, without training and without observing the
now minimal disciplinary procedures! This was touted in some
circles as a great act of "evangelism," but no similar practice could
be found in John Wesley or Francis Asbury; one would have to
go back to Francis Xavier and the baptism of the Malabar coast
fisher people to find a comparable practice. But St. Francis Xavier
was supported by another kind of order and cultic discipline; the
promiscuous acceptance into membership of masses of people is
another matter, and it is in any case destructive of Free Church
discipline and contrary to Wesleyan standards.

It is worth noting that the Southern Baptists, with a similar
background in the period of rapid growth, have like problems.
They too have sacrificed a number of their principles for the
sake of popularity, and in addition in some areas they have been
sufficiently raddled by "child evangelism" to begin the practice
of baptizing children. But the official press of the denomination
has just published a major study of the disciplinary situation by
a professor in the Southern Baptist Theological Seminary. In
A Quest for Vitality in Religion, Findley B. Edge deals sharply
with the general promiscuity of membership standards, the wide-

[6] *The Discipline of the Methodist Episcopal Church* (New York, Eaton
& Mains, 1908), pp. 49, 443, 542.

spread dishonesty in church statistics (which the Baptists share
with the rest of us). He makes excellent suggestions, especially in
Part IV, on how to recover the internal integrity of the Baptist
movement. So far no such soul-searching has been sponsored by
the Methodist Publishing House, nor is it likely that it will be,
under present leadership.

The final irony of the situation is that, in spite of the watered
statistics reported by prominent "pulpiteers," the abandonment
of standards did not open the way to additional statistical gains:
the elimination of membership standards actually inaugurated the
period of declining gains and receding public influence in the
larger Methodist denominations. It also led, unhappily, to
the splitting off of more than twenty smaller churches—such as
the Church of the Nazarene and the Church of God—which were
rightly convinced that the surrender of membership standards for
the sake of social popularity could only mean disaster to the Wesleyan cause. The particular form of their objection to promiscuity
was doctrinal: they charged that the big churches were no longer
preaching the claims of "Christian perfection" and "Scriptural
holiness." Regardless of the form of words, what they were saying
was quite true: the large denomination was sinking rapidly into
the status of a social establishment, of a culture-religion at peace
with the spirit of the times, and this was a betrayal of the heart
and core of Methodism. Whereas John Wesley's progression was
from establishment to disciplined Free Church, the regression of
the large American Methodist bodies has been from separated
peoplehood to social establishment.

II

The most acute crisis confronting the large Protestant churches
today is in the area of disciplined witness, and Methodism thus
enters the battle spiritually disarmed. With the posture and practice of an established church, but without the classical instruments
of instruction and control which grace such traditions as Lutheran-

ism and Anglicanism, the denomination is very far from the effective collective witness to which all Christians are called by virtue of the ordination of their baptism. A large Methodist congregation once justified its promiscuous practices as follows:

. . . What is a church? It certainly isn't a club of saints. We believe it is a fellowship of those who are seeking after righteousness, and we believe that when they knock at the doors of the church, then is the time to swing them open and take them in. Our major responsibility starts once they cross the threshold. Our principle, in other words, isn't exclusion; it's inclusion, and then using every bit of resources we have, both personal and material, to do the best job of Christian nurture of which we are capable.[7]

Whatever else it is, this is the stance of an established church. One minister, in objecting to the author's original appeal for a recovery of discipline, said that no one was taken off the membership rolls of his church for any reason other than transfer or death. In his words:

I am willing to wait all a man's life for him to repent. That maturity which results in responsible action comes early to some, late to others, depending upon the conditions which are peculiar to his life.[8]

This practice is not only well-nigh universal in the Methodist Church: it has been encouraged and authorized by the denominational authorities. It should not have to be argued that to permit persons to attend on the means of grace, and to help run (or misrun) the denomination, while waiting in hope of a Constantinian deathbed conversion, is—whatever its assumed social merits—contrary to Wesleyan understanding of the Christian life. The argument for promiscuous membership practice is precisely that used by the Church of Sweden, the Church of England, the Church of Hannover. But the old established churches of Europe have at least a powerful tradition of public authority, sacramental

[7] *The Christian Century*, LXIX (1952), 46:1315.
[8] Personal correspondence: March 1, 1963.

life, catechetical and confirmation training, and the like, to provide some safeguards against a general apostasy. Even they, in a "post-Christian situation," are today questioning just how successful these safeguards are!

It is appallingly symbolic that the same local church cited above, which has indeed leadership of the highest quality, has recently had an Official Board action attacking denominational and ecumenical leadership for giving leadership on social questions. In other words, promiscuity of membership practice leads finally to the privatization of religion and the attempt to emasculate preaching and witness. But how are the laity to understand the need for separation, for discontinuity with the spirit of the times, if they have never been trained to swim against the stream? Who are at fault when heathenism becomes militant and overt—the sheep without shepherding, or those who sacrificed Methodist standards for the sake of a fleeting show of statistical success?

It is the race issue which above all exposes the nakedness of the Methodist Church. And the burden of reasserting the Lordship of Jesus Christ, the Universal Lord of a Universal Church, falls most heavily upon the Baptists and Methodists. Four out of five Negro Christians in the United States are Baptists; one out of six is a Methodist; one out of thirty is anything else. To date, the Methodists have not even been able to restrain their membership from mob action, violence and anarchy. A few years ago a wicked man stood on the floor of the most powerful legislative body in the world, the United States Senate, and made an obscene attack on fellow-citizens whom he called "niggers and kikes and dagoes." When decent men rose to protest—and one of them died of a heart attack during the incident!—he protested, "I'm a good Christian. . . . I'm a good Methodist." (!) This led the former president of the National Council of Methodist Youth to write:

The Church ought to have sufficient ethical sensitiveness and power to reprimand or to remove from membership persons whose ideas and actions are totally contrary to Christian standards.[9]

[9] Hayes Beall in *The Christian Century*, LXII (1945), 29:840.

Perhaps needless to say, no such reprimand of a United States Senator has been forthcoming. And the person in question has continued his course, building his power in good part by lying about the leaders of our country and its institutions and about the leaders of our churches (including his own). But it can also be said that the reason he has gone without rebuke is that John Wesley and Francis Asbury are long dead, and those who have come after them no longer feel obligated to maintain even what is left of *The Discipline* of the Methodist Church.

At the time of my earlier essay on Methodist indiscipline, a laywoman wrote a wise comment on the situation:

If members were to join the church because of a commitment, it might be proper to hold them accountable to the church for their actions. But many—perhaps most—join because of a desire to conform to an accepted custom. . . . And since the prevailing opinion among respectable people seems to be "it doesn't matter where you go to church—just so you go," the choice of church is often governed by family custom, locale, "friendliness" of the congregation, personality of the minister, etc., rather than an examination of the principles to which the particular sect adheres. It seems to me then that the purpose of the church is not only to seek conversion of members *to* the church, but also to seek conversion of members *in* the church."[10]

Precisely!

The Recovery of Integrity

Apart from promiscuity of membership practices, the most retarding force in the Methodist Church in recent decades has been in the theological area, where most seminaries and agencies have been under the regressive influence of a dogmatic commitment to 19th century liberalism.

A representative excerpt from a leader of the establishment will

[10] Personal correspondence: March 1, 1963.

illustrate the problem. Speaking of the Bible, he retreats to the posture of a universal humanity:

> Our immediate purpose is to call attention to the broad basis in human experience which makes the Bible an irreplaceable book in creative Christian thinking and living.
>
> The authority of the Bible, then, is that of a long-time experience which validated certain moral and spiritual principles.[11]

He patronizes the Word: for none of us can speak from Cloud Nine. Every one of us lives one life, a very limited and particular one. And, in a life faithful or disobedient, each of us dies one death—which is more particular yet! In another place he expresses his generous appreciation of Jesus. The principles of noble and selfless purpose which make Jesus our Leader are outlined as follows:

1. A great personality is organized around a cause which seeks the welfare of many people.
4. A great personality will be characterized by integrity or by unqualified support of the cause.
6. A great personality is distinguished by the ability to enlist the support of other people.[12]

This attitude to the Bible and to Jesus antedates, of course, all ecumenical discussion within recent decades. More serious, it is perfectly in agreement with those of the German Christians (*Deutsche Christen*) who accommodated themselves to Hitler, or with those of the "progressive pastors" who have collaborated with the Communists. In fact, they are the views of those 19th century champions of culture-religion who prepared the way for the rise of contemporary anti-Christian systems. They act in the same way to delete the offense of the gospel, remove the burden

[11] Harold A. Bosley, *On Final Ground* (New York, Harper & Brothers, 1946), pp. 13, 21.
[12] *Ibid.*, pp. 38-39.

of discontinuity with the spirit of the times, and prepare the way for the establishment of a low-grade culture-religion in place of a witnessing people.

With the most significant theological developments of the day both post-Fundamentalist and post-Liberal, this dogmatic commitment of most of the leaders of the Methodist establishment has until recently confronted Methodists who took theological issues seriously with the choice of either abandoning intellectual discipline or getting out of the denomination. A number of younger Methodist theologians have won international distinction, but not as representatives of Wesleyan or Methodist concerns. At a time when the "late bloomers" among the Protestant denominations have produced men of the theological distinction associated with the names Niebuhr, Lehmann, Homrighausen, Sittler, Pelikan *et al.*, there is not one Methodist scholar on the faculties of the four major graduate schools of religion. A generation ago, on Methodist faculties, Edwin Lewis of Drew and George Croft Cell of Boston tried to awaken the church to its theological heritage; but they gained no significant following.

The anti-intellectualism of the Methodist establishment has been enforced by freezing out teachers and writers who are committed to the contemporary revival of theology, although in recent years several Methodist seminaries have assembled faculties of considerable distinction. But it is the self-examination of ecclesiastical commitments, institutional structures, the testing of present practices by that which is valid in the Wesleyan heritage, which has been most ardently opposed in the power centers of the denomination.

The traditional references to excuse intellectual indiscipline have been the sentimentalization of the Aldersgate experience, when Wesley felt his heart strangely warmed, and the short quotation from his letter to Howell Harris:

Brother, is thy heart with mine, as my heart is with thy heart? If it be, give me thy hand. . . .

But Wesley's real conversion was not Aldersgate: it was when he determined to break clean from culture-religion and freely use field preaching to win followers on a voluntary basis. And a fuller selection from the letter to Harris would reveal that Wesley never sacrificed basic commitments in theology and action:

. . . We agree (1) that no man can have any power except it be given him from above; (2) that no man can merit anything but hell, seeing all other merit is in the blood of the Lamb. . . . Why then, . . . what need of this great gulf to be fixed between us? Brother, is thy heart with mine, as my heart is with thy heart? If it be, give me thy hand. . . . Let us rise up together against the evildoers. Let us not weaken, but (if it be our Lord's will) strengthen one another's hands in God.[13]

Over a generation there has been a major leakage from Methodism to other denominations, both among the clergy and among seminary professors. Wesley himself would have been horrified at the anti-intellectual and anti-theological bent in the establishment, which is largely responsible for these defections.

George Croft Cell was certainly correct, when he wrote for an older generation which was deaf to his message:

Wesley in the epoch of his maturity was never an Arminian as that term is now more commonly taken and accepted. Wesley would reject as decisively the current Arminianism of Methodist theology today as he rejected the current Arminianism of Anglican theology of his own time and for the same reasons. As he saw it, Anglican theology, decidedly Arminian, had "run from Calvinism as far as ever it could," whereas "the truth of the Gospel lies within a hair's breadth of Calvin." Anglican teaching and preaching had in its anti-Calvinist animus broken so radically with the religious principles of the Reformation that it had simply ceased to be evangelical. It no longer had a gospel to preach, certainly not one which is the power of God unto salvation

[13] In Richard M. Cameron, *The Rise of Methodism: A Source Book* (New York, Philosophical Library, 1943), p. 316.

to every believer. Wesley, therefore, after exploring this Arminian
theology for over ten years, concluded that it was a byway of spiritual
despair and futility, not a highway of saving faith and Christian perfection, and went back in his search for power to the Luther-Calvin
idea of a God-given faith.[14]

Whether Arminius himself would have been pleased with what
some later generations have called "Arminianism" is doubtful. But
there is no doubt whatever as to what he and John Wesley would
have thought of the outright Pelagianism of much of contemporary Methodism!

For Methodist scholars concerned for the Methodist heritage
the most frustrating problem is to be closed off from any lively
discussion of basic issues within the church. On occasion, some
editors of journals—particularly the lively group associated with
The Christian Advocate—have felt free to publish articles which
strike a discordant note and raise questions about our current
complacency. But the basic problem remains: the lack of a high-
grade theoretical journal for the discussion of major historical and
theological problems. For example, a group of men has for several
years been pushing for the founding of a *Methodist Review*. This
journal would function the way earlier reviews of that name had
served the M. E. Church and M. E. Church, South, before unification. In other denominations seeking to rethink their self-image
and the image of their mission in contemporary America, there
have appeared significant fraternal and ecumenical journals: *Theology Today*, *The Mennonite Quarterly Review*, *Foundations*,
Encounter, *Brethren Life and Thought*, etc. When the faculties
of the twelve Methodist seminaries met in Nashville in 1960—for
the first time!—they passed only one resolution, and that unanimously: a request to the Board of Education and the Publishing
House for the founding of such a journal. So far the recommenda-
tion has been successfully suppressed.

[14] George Croft Cell, *The Rediscovery of John Wesley* (New York,
Henry Holt & Co., 1935), p. 25.

III

Finally, professionals can clear the way for a recovery of
theological and liturgical integrity, but the renewal of the church
at all levels can only occur through the recovery of the laity—
"God's Frozen People"[15] and the witness of the whole believing
people. When the lay people tire sufficiently of empty "pulpiteer-
ing," of verbiage without the quality of bindingness, then the
recovery of disciplined witness will proceed apace in Methodism
—as elsewhere in Christendom.

John Wesley once said that to win people without providing
them with the means of grace was "but to breed children for the
Murderer." He was referring particularly to the Class Meeting,
that Methodist "fellowship group" or "house church" in which
the newly-won learned the fundamentals of Christian belief and
practice, in which older members learned to grow in grace and
in sturdiness of witness, and in which both learned the "separation"
which marks the Christian style of life from that affirmed by the
spirit of the times. The genius of the small primary group is that
it is the maximal training unit—the unit within which persons can
"learn the most the fastest," and use it best under pressure. Rightly
conceived, such a group is a "dialogue" group: that is, by the free
sharing of questions and concerns, among persons united with
"the open face of truth," the basis is laid for a new and voluntary
covenant of Christian discipline and witness. Although it is certainly appropriate to judge present lassitude by reference to past
standards of Methodist discipline, the simple recovery of old
structures is neither possible nor desirable. What is needed, in
full discussion among those present and concerned, and with a
full regard to the testimony of those who have died in the faith,
is a renewal of the church's ministry (Ephesians 4).

There are several places where lay people and concerned

---

[15] An excellent book of this title, on the laity, has just been published by
two members of the Iona Community: Mark Gibbs and Ralph T. Morton
(London, Fontana Books, 1964).

pastors are attempting to recover a program of instruction and Christian discipline. It would be invidious to single out names, but it should be said that the Methodist Student Movement has contributed greatly to the recovery of integrity of churchmanship. And the Indiana Area, under able episcopal leadership and with the assistance of staff and program facilities at Yokefellow Institute (Richmond), has done a remarkable work in recent years of putting content into church membership at the local level. In other sectors, however, there is evidence that a low-grade anti-Catholicism is being used to recover an easy identity without the real spiritual struggle which the recovery of internal integrity and disciplined witness would require. It is appallingly symbolic that the same General Conference (Denver, 1960) which forbade the removal of dead wood from the membership rolls for at least five years should have approved the appropriation of monies to support the anti-Catholic propaganda of "the collegeman's KKK" (POAU)! Here we have the real watershed choice for Methodism (and for much of American Protestantism): either a renewal of evangelical commitment and discipline *or* a reversion to more and more embittered culture-religion.[16]

It is the movement of renewal at the level of the local church or student congregation which, in the long view, is the most promising sign in the Methodist picture. Although it is often opposed by some boards and agencies and promotional programs in the mistaken belief that statistical success and qualitative gains are mutually exclusive, there is a marked groundswell of determination to release the frozen assets of Methodism: a committed and trained apostolate of the laity. With the steady recovery of disciplined witness by the whole body of believers, it may be hoped that the need for an anxiously cultivated hostility to other communions will disappear, and that a rebirth of authentic Christian joy and Wesleyan evangelicalism may occur.

[16] Cf. "The Usefulness of Anti-Catholicism," *The Commonweal*, LXXVIII (1963), 16:422-24.

7. THE UNITED CHURCH OF CANADA: PERILS OF ECCLESIASTICISM

Ernest Marshall Howse*

The United Church of Canada is the result of a union, consummated in 1925, of Congregational, Methodist and Presbyterian churches. The entire constituency of the Methodist and Congregational churches of Canada entered the union. The Presbyterian Church, by heavy majority vote in all its courts, entered the union *as a church*. But a minority (17 per cent) of the Presbyterian congregations, almost all of them in eastern Canada, voted against union and remained outside.

At the time of union the United Church's communicant membership totaled 623,648; by the end of 1961 that number had increased to 1,036,936. According to Canada's 1961 census, the denomination's total constituency amounted to 3,664,208, slightly more than one-fifth of all Canadians. In the western provinces United Church members constitute one-third of the population. A church comprising so large a segment of the nation's people cannot be isolated from national changes as though it were a small body to be found in limited geographical areas, or as though it were distinctively either urban or rural.

I

The United Church has 253 missionaries at work around the world—in Hong Kong, Brazil, Northern Rhodesia, Angola, India, Japan, Korea and Trinidad. The diversity of its operations is partly explained by the fact that the uniting churches had mis-

* Dr. Howse is pastor of Bloor Street United Church, Toronto.

sions in different areas. The United Church's missionary program,
already radically changed, is bound to be changed still more. Individual missions, operated independently by one denomination
from one country, rightly should disappear. In the future such
missionary enterprise of the church as remains possible may very
well be conducted through the World Council of Churches, in
cooperation with the Christians to whose assistance the missionaries go.

Within Canada the United Church, while not limited to rural
areas, has been mainly a rural church. Two-thirds of its ministers
have spent their lives in rural congregations, and one-fourth of its
2,175 pastoral charges are still aid-receiving home missions. Each
summer the denomination's Home Mission Board augments its
regular work by sending 250 student missionaries to remote new
settlements where services cannot be regularly maintained through
the winter. In the cities the United Church has, in addition to its
regular congregations, a chain of community centers, institutional
churches and churches of all nations. United Church ministers
preach the gospel on Sunday in 20 languages, do pastoral work
in 30.

II

The United Church faces problems and anomalies that are
distinctively Canadian. Apart from Quebec province, Canada in
the past has been predominantly a Protestant country, with a
Protestant majority and a Protestant ethos. Today the total
Canadian population is 46 per cent Roman Catholic. Immigrants
now come mainly from predominantly Catholic countries—if for
causes not primarily religious—and Canada will soon have a
Catholic majority. Moreover, at the time of its confederation
Canada made certain legal commitments to the Roman Catholic
Church. The consequences to both Catholics and Protestants have
been complicated and perplexing.

Two Canadian provinces—Quebec and Newfoundland—have

no public schools; there the provincial governments support the denominational schools. In Newfoundland not only do Roman Catholic children go to Roman Catholic schools but Anglican children go to Anglican schools, United Church children to United Church schools—and sometimes Salvation Army children to Salvation Army schools. In Quebec all non-Catholic youth, whether Protestant or not, attend the "Protestant" schools.

Ontario has long had primary-level parochial schools. In recent years such schools, under the vigorous promotion of the Roman Catholic clergy, have increased rapidly. In the fall of 1962 the 20 Roman Catholic bishops of Ontario province sent a formal brief to members of the provincial parliament demanding Catholic high schools, technical schools and teachers colleges, to be supported by the state in the same way as the public schools, "the sole distinction between the two being that the Roman Catholic separate school shall be conducted in accordance with Roman Catholic exigencies." The bishops called for a complete system of state-supported Catholic schools in which teachers, trained separately in state-supported Catholic colleges, would develop "a true Catholic philosophy of life."

The demand for parochial high schools, technical schools and teachers colleges was denied. But substantial increases were made in the monies allotted to parochial primary schools. The public schools trustee association protested that the new grants meant that, though parochial schools enroll only 25.9 per cent of all Ontario elementary school pupils, they will get 29.7 per cent of the provincial school funds. A Catholic bishop said that the problem of aid to Catholic high schools had not been met, but that the new grants constituted "a step forward."

Many Canadians fear that, in Ontario and elsewhere, other "steps forward" under persistent political pressure may well lead to the disintegration of the public schools. Protestants are in sympathy with Catholics' desire for education not deliberately secular in underlying philosophy, and it is conceivable that the two groups might be able to work out an agreement on the order of the "shared time" programs now gaining ground in the

United States, with approval from many U.S. Catholics. But
Protestants fear that the long-term goals of the Roman church,
as revealed in the demands of the bishops, indicate that more
trouble may be in store for Canadian education.

III

In higher education, too, the United Church encounters problems distinctively Canadian in character. At the university level
federal grants have since 1952 paid approximately 30 per cent of
each student's education costs. These grants are allotted to the
various universities according to the number of students working
toward a degree, and without regard to their field of study. Thus
both United Church ministers and Roman Catholic priests have
part of their education paid for by federal funds.

The United Church operates three universities, one college,
eight theological seminaries, eight secondary schools and a training school for deaconesses. But the denomination's institutions also
have influence in the universities which are independent or
provincial. Its Victoria University in Toronto, for example, is
one of a group of universities and colleges which together constitute the University of Toronto. The latter grants the degrees
and controls the standards. But in the setting of standards and the
formation of policy Victoria University, like the participating
Roman Catholic and Anglican colleges, has a voice. Thus the
United Church will continue to share in the shaping of the character of Canadian university education.

The complexities of the Canadian religious scene are not limited
to the field of education. Canada is rapidly being transformed
from a sparsely settled rural country into an industrialized society
dominated by a chain of metropolitan centers. Each year one
Canadian family in four relocates. In the midst of such change
the United Church is finding its center of gravity violently
disturbed.

In the past the great congregations in the cities were sustained
and augmented by an influx of members from small country

churches. Now the rural areas are rapidly diminishing. The suburbs—still largely Protestant—sprawl in endless miles from the metropolitan centers, and in the cities themselves Protestant churches are becoming islands in the midst of an ever expanding Roman Catholic constituency.

The patterns of church work in urban, suburban and rural areas all need to be radically revised. Too many city churches remain mired in past traditions, passively if anxiously preserving their impoverished status quo. Too many suburban churches are operating with one minister, on the pattern of the "little red schoolhouse." Too many country churches, built but a few miles apart because in pioneer days congregations reached them in buggies along deep-rutted dirt roads, jealously perpetuate their individual existence—though the only ruts remaining are in the mind.

At present the United Church suffers from a shortage of ministers. It has prospect of only 105 to 110 ordinations per year, providing, after retirements are taken into account, a net gain of 25—a number far from commensurate with the rate of church expansion. But the shortage may be an artificial one—one which would vanish if the charges were reorganized with deference to modern conditions instead of to grandfather's grave or Aunt Susie's memorial font.

IV

Whatever the pattern of change, the United Church cannot permit itself to abandon any significant area of community life. It cannot be content to become the church of the upper middle class, operating at a few strategic missions to the down and out. It cannot countenance leaving a wasteland between the downtown city mission and the comfortable outlying suburb. Very likely the denomination will have to move toward new patterns of organization in its rural ministry, and, in the cities and suburbs, toward something resembling the Roman Catholic pattern, with larger units making available a more specialized ministry. Industrial chaplains, hospital chaplains, community centers may be future agents of the church's evangelism.

The future of the United Church of Canada may be further affected by the nature of the denomination's ecclesiastical administration, accentuated by its peculiar geographical setting. Even today Canada is largely a ribbon of population 4,000 miles long and 100 miles wide, with streamers running here and there to the north. Along that ribbon the United Church is divided into 11 conferences and 101 presbyteries in which—even in 1963— 2,225 of its pastoral charges have fewer than 500 members.

The church's presbyteries meet throughout the year, in the northern areas perhaps only in fall and spring. The conferences —analogous to Presbyterian synods, but with wider powers— meet annually. For economic reasons the General Council, the church's supreme court, usually holds its biennial meeting in an eastern city, though it has gone to Vancouver and is slated to go next to Newfoundland. The General Council directs policy and establishes legislation. Its outreach is channeled through ten administrative boards and 18 standing committees.

So far the United Church has found no satisfactory way to give its General Council a representation as wide as is desirable and at the same time as experienced as is necessary for wise dispatch of its business. Of the 390 commissioners present at the General Council meeting last September, only 14 ministerial and 16 nonministerial commissioners had attended the previous council. The next council will probably register just as few who attended the previous one. This is not the best way to establish continuity of judgment in a supreme court.

The situation is complicated by the fact that the council's agenda generally runs to almost 800 printed pages; also, it is issued to commissioners only, and to them less than a month before the meeting convenes. This agenda presents the findings of boards and commissions; its lengthy reports often bury in verbosity recommendations calling for highly significant legislative changes. The persons who present these reports at the meeting generally consume most of their allotted time in summarizing the printed text. Then come the resolutions—the significance of which many of the commissioners may not have previously noted—followed by a hurried few moments of debate. With the narrowest of margins a vote can change a long-established policy or program, though the majority of church ministers and members have had no hint that such a proposal was even mooted.

It would be unjust to charge the men and women who work on reports and commissions, and in particular the individuals who happen to present the reports, with any desire to flout the will of the church at large. They are caught in the web of the church's general pattern. But unless the United Church can develop some method of seeking the consensus of the church as a whole before permitting significant changes to be made in its manual, successive General Councils will accumulate a muddle of mandatory regulations which do not carry general consent and which will be widely resented or ignored. Unhappily, the United Church is exhibiting symptoms of an ecclesiastical catatonia ("negativism, incoherence . . . with alternate periods of stupor and activity") which, had it existed in the uniting churches, would have effectively stalled the movement toward union.

Curiously, the development of ecclesiasticism in the United Church is in part the outcome of its concern for the ecumenical movement. We must not do this or that, we are cautioned, because by doing so we will make it harder for the Orthodox or the Anglicans to acknowledge that we are a true church. But if we put on heavier ecclesiastical robes, if we refuse to marry divorced persons whom their own church will not marry or to ordain women who have been married, if we recite the creed more frequently, then, it seems to many, we are really doing our part to move the ecumenical bandwagon.

V

This criticism is not, however, an adequate report on the spiritual life of the United Church of Canada. The nature of the denomination's spiritual life is difficult to assess, the development of that life difficult to predict. Some observers believe that the United Church, which in its earlier days was necessarily occupied with institutional structures, is now showing deeper concern for its spiritual foundations. Dr. Ralph Chalmers of Pine Hill Seminary, for example, says that in the United Church there has been a remarkable upsurge of theological interest and something of a renaissance in biblical theology. In this new emphasis, asserts Dr. Chalmers, "we have placed ourselves more fully in the stream of the Christian verities, which have found expression in the Christian's creeds and confessions, and which need to be stressed in new forms and ways in each generation." Dr. George Johnston of Montreal is more skeptical. He sees signs of a theological revival, but, looking at its forms of expression, he is not sure whether the United Church has had "a decent dose of theological adrenalin" or "a mild case of hardening of theological arteries." Dr. J. S. Thomson, a former moderator of the denomination, sees "a growing tendency to bureaucracy and centralization."

Leadership of the United Church is now passing from men who came from the uniting churches to men who are products of the denomination. The former leaders knew what they believed, if only because they wanted to assure survival of their belief in the new union. The outlook of the men now coming to positions of leadership is far removed from that of their more sanguine predecessors. But as yet there are no clear indications whether the United Church will move into a wider freedom of mind and a more powerful dynamic of spirit, or into a more constricting orthodoxy and a more heavy-handed bureaucracy.

In one particular the United Church has so far met with disappointment. At its birth almost forty years ago it proclaimed its desire to be not only a united but a uniting church; however, its great hopes have had little result. Since union the United Church has received into its fold several small groups—the Wesleyan United Church of Bermuda, for example—as well as congregations from the Christian Church and from the Evangelical and Reformed Church. It is now engaged in discussions with the

Evangelical United Brethren and the Disciples. But there seems no immediate prospect of further unions with larger denominations. In Canada Baptists and Lutherans are still too few and too divided not to fear being swallowed by a large national church. Stumbling blocks in the road to unity with the Anglican Church seem impassable. But there is no reason, creditable to Christian faith, for further evading negotiations with the section of the Presbyterian Church which eschewed the union of a generation ago.

The United Church, it seems to this critic from within, is riddled with faults and deficiencies. Multitudes of its members affront its spirit or serve it with little zeal and less knowledge. But the unremarked 7,000, or some number noted only in the heraldry of heaven, still preserve the devotion and the spirit of adventure which marked their pioneering sires. The Canada of the future will be vastly different from that of the past. But in that Canada the United Church, changed and changing still, will endure, a source of spiritual influence to be measured only in the arithmetic of God.

8. THE PEACE CHURCHES AS COMMUNITIES OF DISCERNMENT

J. Lawrence Burkholder*

Instead of trying to chart a common course for three distinct denominations viewed in their entirety (an impossible task!) I will arbitrarily limit myself to consideration of a single problem facing the peace churches—one which a small but significant

* A former Mennonite missionary, Dr. Burkholder is now professor of pastoral theology at Harvard Divinity School.

group of Quaker, Church of the Brethren and Mennonite theologians and sociologists are attacking with youthful radicality. The problem is centered in the structure of the local congregation: How can today's congregation be designed in order to express the underlying intentions of faith as interpreted by the peace churches? Serious doubts are being expressed about the uncritical way in which the peace churches have borrowed from many of the institutional structures of mainline Protestantism—some of which are being called into question by traditional Protestant churches themselves. Furthermore, certain peace church practices which have become vestigial are now seen to be the very ones which may enable the Body to live. They need to be reinterpreted and reinstated in a total congregational morphology. Hence new structures are being sought and actual experiments are under way.

The fact that certain members of the peace churches are facing this problem together may be explained by the recent consciousness of a common ecclesiological substratum upon which to build. Beneath the obvious differences between the Quaker meeting and the Brethren and Mennonite congregation lies a set of similar assumptions about what the church is and the place that it should occupy in the lives of its members. Probably the uniqueness of the peace churches lies not so much in espousal of pacifism as in the concept of the congregation within which their pacifism is grounded. Discipline, lay responsibility, simplicity, service and spiritual discernment are just a few of the traditional practices which unite them in common cause. Probably the greatest contribution that the peace churches can make to Christendom lies in the area of the concept of the congregation. But this concept must be reinterpreted and made to work under the conditions of modern life.

The search for new forms of congregational organization comes at a time when the peace churches seem to be in the mood to experiment. They are on the move; the question is, where will they go? Admittedly, many congregations will resist change for years to come. But certain facts about the nature of tradition in the peace churches tend to limit its power. For them tradition is primarily neither institutional nor theological, as it is among many denominations; it is in substance cultural, and this means that it may be challenged by cultural relativity.

Furthermore, the peace churches have no one fixed polity. Mennonite bishops have sometimes exercised considerable power, but this is to be attributed to historical accident rather than to episcopal dogma. Creeds are not the "teaching of the church"; rather, they are periodic confessions of faith of which there are many. A biblicism which once stifled change is becoming, under the influence of historical criticism, the basis for spirit-directed change. One of the salutary effects of biblically oriented faith is the freedom to adapt to unexpected situations in the manner of the New Testament churches. And by coincidence many of the ideas of the empirical scientists concerning social organization resemble secularized versions of New Testament koinonia. The crust of historic tradition among the peace churches is breaking; the alluvial soil of faith is now exposed to the winds and the rains of modernity. What new topographical forms lie ahead?

I

It would be premature to suggest where the search for new forms of congregational life may lead. But the search for "models" is on, in a manner not unlike the search for models in science. The best one can do at this stage is to suggest a model by selecting ideas from the discussion on the basis of one's own biased opinion. A model is of course multidimensional and cannot be sketched completely here. Nevertheless, the following may indicate how one pivotal dimension of congregational life can be shaped.

The dimension of congregational life I propose to treat is ethical responsibility. According to certain traditional peace church views, the Bible's "binding and loosing" references imply that congregations must be structured to function as ethical communities—to make ethical decisions and to implement them in the world. The challenge before the peace churches and indeed before the theological disciplines of Christian ethics and practical theology is to show concretely how a congregation may become what some of us prefer to call a "discerning community."

The crux of the matter is the decision-making process. How can congregations be structured to make ethical decisions? What are the steps in the formation of a congregational mind? How can the scattered moral sentiments of the members be gathered, informed, disciplined, and concerted in action?

The practical failure of typical congregations in America—including those of the peace churches—to decide and to act corporately is one of the clues to the ethical blandness of Protestantism. Most churches simply do not know how to come to conclusions about things that matter. Nor do they see decision-making as one of the marks of the church. It is assumed that everyone will make up his own mind independently of the congregation. While this attitude reflects an important truth, there are certain problems which by reason of their importance and public character require the decision of the Body of Christ. Unfortunately, the spirit of individualism is so dominant and discernment of the Body so vague that the local church generally squanders its collective power potential. Consensus is seldom sought; discussions are mere forums, and in most cases are not intended to lead to binding commitments; controversial issues are avoided. Dialogical give-and-take, as an instrument of the Holy Spirit, is discouraged by those who prefer "peace" and by those who operate under the illusion that clerical pronouncements are a sufficient substitute for consensus. Is it too harsh to say that most Protestant congregations decide in the course of a year almost nothing of real spiritual importance? The closest they come to consensus is to adopt a budget and to dispose of other matters dictated by administrative necessity. Great issues such as war, race, housing, capital punishment, unemployment and the needs of the underdeveloped countries may be the subjects of sermons, but they do not become

existential realities for most churchmen until they are presented
as issues concerning which the church must make decisions.

II

The call for the discerning community must be seen in relation
to a fundamental change in the cultural situation of the peace
churches—especially that of the Brethren and the Mennonites.
Almost overnight the cultural context has shifted from rural isolation to urban involvement. No longer is Brethren and Mennonite
life a rural phenomenon. Mennonites and Brethren are clear that
from now on the city is the fundamental sociological context of
their churches.

As a result of this change the ethical problems facing the peace
churches are also changing. Such problems are no longer in the
order of adjudication of fence lines. They are highly complicated
and specialized, arising out of business and professional life. They
are less personal and more abstract. Frequently they involve the
delicate balancing of conflicting claims and the rights of power
blocs. More often than not a "third party" is involved in the
situation—which renders inadequate certain favorite biblical texts
which imply a simple face-to-face relation. Furthermore, the educational and psychological composition of many congregations is
changing. Ethical attitudes are becoming more sophisticated as
the educational level rises and as backgrounds become more highly
differentiated. Secular associations are becoming more numerous
and demanding. The church is no longer the unchallenged authority on all matters of importance. The great centers of secular
power can no longer be ignored; they are the apparent powers
of the age and must be seen in Christian perspective.

The challenge is to refuse to surrender to the potentially disin-
tegrating forces of modernity. The peace churches must discover
structures which will actually utilize the rich and varied new
perspectives within the congregation as materials for decision-
making rather than as reasons for retreating into religious in-

dividualism, whether pietistic or liberal. Ironically, some of the earliest practices in Quaker, Brethren and Mennonite history commend themselves today as the ones likely to prove adequate to the new situation. Many of these are being discussed in the current flood of literature on the renewal of the church. Such ideas as discipline, house churches, prayer cells, study groups, lay preaching and missions are indigenous to the peace churches (though it is somewhat disquieting to find peace church people reading the latest on house churches as if they were discoveries of the 20th century!).

Congregations restructured as discerning communities would concertedly seek to meet specific needs in the world. Ethical involvement would be one of the most important ways in which people of faith answer the call to discipleship. Their particular orientation in the area of ethics would not dispose them to sponsor internal exercises in perfection; rather, the congregation would be ordered around works of love in lowly places. Its eyes would be turned outward. Discernment is the way by which a congregation understands its task. The identity of the congregation would not be first of all geographical (the parish principle) nor historical (the denominational principle) nor dogmatic (the sectarian principle). Its identity would be established by what it "does" in a local situation in the world. Worship, fellowship, sacraments, teaching and discipline would belong to the life of the congregation, but these would not be detached from specific ministries. To the outsider such a congregation would look more like a local Peace Corps unit or a closely related set of such units than a band of worshipers. The church building would reflect the modesty of faith rather than the imperial character of Christendom. It would be a headquarters for a number of missions or "task forces," each such entity operating essentially as the church, i.e., as a serving, worshiping, disciplining fellowship. The congregation would thus be primarily an assembly of mission fellowships, not an assembly of individuals. Membership would depend largely on willingness to pay the price of radical discipleship. Not everyone would join such a church, but the basis for exclusion would be preferable to that which is now used in many "inclusive" churches.

III

This is not the place to describe the idea of the discerning community in detail. However, several structural lines may be drawn. For example, the basic decision-making instrument would be the "congregational" meeting. Congregational meetings would be called monthly, possibly more frequently. Important matters which could not be handled in a less time-consuming way would be presented in open forum. Topics would range from theological issues to world affairs—just so they were important. Discussion would be "ordered" according to a theology of discussion (*Gespräch*), and this theology would contain elements of the Quaker tradition of spiritual guidance, the Mennonite tradition of scriptural authority and the Brethren tradition of fellowship. Discussion would be considered just as "spiritual" as preaching and no less central to the congregation's life. "Dialogue" would be conceived as an avenue through which the Holy Spirit speaks. Members would listen not just to one another but to the Holy Spirit who may speak through them. The congregation would live "under" the Bible, while employing critical methods of interpretation. Willingness to "give counsel and receive counsel" —a traditional Mennonite baptismal vow—would be part of the discipline. Since it is unrealistic to assume that agreement is inevitable, honest dissent would be acknowledged with honor and with recourse to later discussion.

The congregation would be relatively small. Factors governing its size would include the number required to accomplish the specific tasks at hand, the natural limits within which depth-communication is possible, and the distribution of leadership. The important thing is that the size of the congregation would be deliberately regulated.

Furthermore, preaching would be shared regularly by the

laity, and adult theological education would be emphasized more than the education of children. The office of the "teacher"— revived from its biblical and New England parish somnolence —would be held by a trained theologian. Religious instruction for the children would be scheduled during the week—a class or so each day, in one or two classrooms. The money that would ordinarily be used for an educational wing large enough to accommodate the congregation's entire offspring could be used to pay the salary of the resident theologian. Religious instruction would be no less rigorous than public school education.

The exact mission of the congregation would be determined by the "needs" of the world round about and the "gifts" within the church. No two congregations would look alike, just as no two Quaker service units do exactly the same thing. Standard organizational charts would be ignored, as would the usual criteria for success. The work of the congregation would be governed largely by the pressure of needs from outside its walls. Finding the right tasks to perform would require an intimate knowledge of the community. The difference between mere do-goodism and significant service is in part the care with which congregations select projects which are crucial yet within their competence. Care should be taken not to duplicate the efforts of capable secular agencies. In many cases churches should concentrate on projects which are aimed at arousing public responsibility. Studies have shown that with the growth of institutions, barriers to communication arise so that people often live in the immediate vicinity of prisons, mental institutions, schools and slum areas without knowing what goes on inside. Right action requires extraordinary understanding of the people and the powers behind and within these institutions.

IV

What lies behind the search for the discerning community is the impact of cultural relativity upon the peace churches. Many people within the peace churches are now facing the full force of cultural relativity for the first time. In overseas relief projects, mission work, mental health clinics, in business and professional life, the peace churches are encountering a cultural "quiltwork" of customs and values. Naturally, this encounter has ethical implications. Some practices which were previously undergirded by biblical authority must now be seen as figments of a rural mentality. The bold line which separates the church from the world must be reinterpreted and redrawn. Existing conceptions of the concrete form the Christian life will take in the world must be reshaped.

In the face of the problem of cultural relativity the peace churches are tempted to move in one of two seemingly opposite directions—both of them tragic. The first is pietism of the popular sort that emphasizes inner religious experience at the expense of the social implications of discipleship. There are just enough similarities between certain virtues and vices of the peace churches and so-called "evangelical" religion to make the latter appear viable. Fundamentalist theology and missionary zeal tend to serve some people as a kind of compensation for the loss of a distinctive Christian ethic.

The other direction is secularism. Secularism among the peace churches would take the form not of outright criticism of the Christian faith but of a "Christian" ethic in which the living Christ is no longer crucial. In such an ethic obedience to his personal command would be replaced by sheer pragmatic calculation. Ethical decisions would be routinized to such an extent that Christ's lordship would tend to be subsumed by the historical process and his purposes identified with the highest intentions of Western society. Christ's freedom to break into the historical process and to command his church to accept a path of obedience which transcends ordinary expectations of goodness and duty would be theologically conceivable but practically unexpected. This is not, of course, to suggest that pragmatic calculation has no place in Christian ethics or that every decision must be accompanied by a revelation. Rather it is to say that unless the

peace churches can hear within the realities of history a concrete
command which they believe to be the command of the Lord,
the quality of ethics which brought those churches into existence
will be lost.

V

On the surface the foregoing may appear to suggest that the
peace churches are simply struggling with the current issue between absolutism and relativism, or between an ethic of principles
as over against a kind of contextualism. This is part of the picture
but not the problem at its deepest level. Suffice to say, principles
and contexts are, respectively, noetic and historical necessities,
and as such should both be a part of decision-making. The crucial
problem facing the churches is that not of making a choice between the two but of determining how principles and contexts
may be seen in relation to the living Lord. Principles without
Christ result in deadly legalism; contextualism without the living
Word ends in untrammeled relativism.

The challenge before the peace churches is to become discerning congregations which "test" whether the authenticating reality
of the obedient life is present today, i.e., whether there is a word
from the Lord. Such congregations would seek to learn how to
"listen" so that if a word is spoken it may be heard with joy and
obedience. Christian ethics, so far as theoretical considerations are
concerned, would be primarily descriptive of how the Word has
been discerned within the work and fellowship of the congregation. If Christ does not become a living reality within the congregation, then it would appear misleading to discuss problems
that presume that he has. Better admit quite frankly that the peace
churches are not certain about what constitutes obedience today
and that Christian ethics in the deepest sense does not exist among
them.

The call for reality in ethics so conceived is dangerous, but it
is unavoidable within the terms which the peace churches have

traditionally set for themselves. Having shunned many of the norms of "religion" and culture in deference to the Word of Christ, they must, for the sake of the integrity of their faith, do what can be done in our time to discern that Word. The discerning community would thereby bring the truth of cultural relativity and the spirit of Christ into creative interaction.

9. FORMULA IN FLUX: REFORMATION FOR THE DISCIPLES OF CHRIST?

Ronald E. Osborn*

The peculiar chemistry of the Christian Churches (Disciples of Christ) is an unstable compound of tradition represented by the formula RFU: R = Restoration of primitive Christianity; F = Freedom in Christ; U = Union of all Christians.

The 19th century American frontier provided conditions under which that formula generated great spiritual power, but in the 20th century it has proved increasingly unstable. Though various attempts have been made to combine the elements in differing proportions (RF_9U_4, RF_4U_7) or to concentrate on one or two of the elements, washing the others out, discomfiture has been the recent lot of Disciples as the tradition simmered in uneasy flux. Will a new formula capable of stability emerge in our time? A study of the old RFU formulation will help to answer that question.

I

R. Restoration of the apostolic church was a goal virtually axiomatic for many Protestants a century and a half ago. What

* Dr. Osborn is dean of Christian Theological Seminary in Indianapolis.

emerged in the particular Disciple expression of the principle was simon-pure congregationalism, with no connectional structure. The church and its members were called by biblical names— Church of Christ, Christian Church, Church of God, Disciples, Christians and so on. Baptism was by immersion of penitent believers. The Lord's Supper was observed every Sunday under the ministry of local elders as the essential feature of Christian worship. Disciples firmly believed that they were "taking the country" with their reasonable, biblical, Christ-centered faith.

F. Freedom was the supreme value on the frontier, and the early Disciples sought to guarantee it negatively by rejecting creeds, connectional church structure, speculative theology and an educated professional ministry. The positive side of freedom appeared in the initiative of individual Disciples in starting thousands of churches, hundreds of religious journals, and scores of colleges (many of which soon collapsed). The deepest fear about any new development these days—whether toward church union or toward strengthening the denomination's own institutions—is not that it may be unscriptural but that it may pose a threat to the freedom and the opportunity for responsible initiative which Disciples so earnestly cherish.

U. At the beginning, union of Christians was the avowed goal; restoration was the means of achieving it; guarantee of freedom was the assurance of inclusiveness. Denominationalism was reprehended not only as unscriptural but also as viciously severing the body of Christ. The strategy for Christian union was to dissolve all ecclesiastical structure and let local congregations take their stand on the Bible alone as churches of Christ supporting one another in brotherly affection. It was precisely this process that marked the emergence of the Disciples as a "particular people," convinced that as frontier presbyteries and Baptist associations dissolved, all Christians would sink into "union with the body of Christ at large."

The irony was that these Disciples who sought unity on "the divine pattern" with a biblical name soon became a sect "everywhere spoken against." The movement grew by evangelism or proselytism, with little distinction drawn between the two. The ideal of unity, Disciples felt, would be realized when "the plea" had swept the Christian world. Sectarian as this attitude was, they never ceased to pray in the words of John 17; today their most responsive nerve is touched by the words "Christian unity."

II

Was the original formula, after all, plain RFU? Disciples have tended to think so. I should say that from 1830 to 1900 the formula was really R_3F_2U, if not $R_{10}F_{10}U$. It may be that in many instances the U element escaped entirely, except for a lingering fragrance of sanctity. But such a charge must not be brought against all members of the denomination. Even in the most sectarian period of their history, when Disciples lived in spiritual and intellectual isolation from the rest of Christendom, there were great minds and spirits among them who continued to think, often with originality and daring, in catholic and ecumenical terms. Before 1900, however, scarcely anyone would have departed from the RFU formula, with the R retaining at least equal value with each of the other elements.

The 20th century demonstrated the instability of the formula and left Disciples wondering where to turn.

R. It is the element of restoration that has proved most troublesome. By 1906 the federal census of religious bodies registered a division between moderates (Disciples of Christ) and absolutists (Churches of Christ). The absolutists rejected such "innovations" as missionary societies and the use of musical instruments in worship.

Almost at once the outlines of a second schism began to appear. Restorationists who had accepted the missionary society as a legitimate expedient stumbled at the new attitude emerging among Disciples of openness to "the denominations"; they considered membership in the Federal Council of Churches and comity on the mission field a compromise in fundamentals. Far more explosive was their concern over the growing practice of "open membership," the reception of baptized but unimmersed persons from other communions by transfer without immersion. In 1927 the restorationists launched a separate convention—a regular assembly of churches. We now have in the restorationist camp "loyal" or "independent" or "direct support" missionaries, Bible colleges, youth camps, publishing enterprises. Although no final schism has been acknowledged, today one can readily identify individual ministers as "cooperative" or "independent." Generally speaking, urban churches and congregations with a full-time, seminary-educated ministry are cooperative. For the independents the formula tends to emerge as plain RF.

Meanwhile among cooperative Disciples, who think of themselves as the "main body," restorationism has been fatally weakened. Within the past twenty-five years the "functional system of church organization" has become a virtual mark of orthodoxy; it was developed on pragmatic, not restorationist terms. The biblical and theological scholarship of recent decades has made restorationism untenable; it has destroyed the mentality within which restorationism flourished. As a result the characteristic practices of Disciples are now rationalized purely on grounds of freedom and of ecumenical significance or—to an astounding degree—of tradition. Most Disciples who have repudiated restorationism have no adequate basis for justifying their congregationalism, weekly communion, immersion-baptism, boards of elders and deacons (vestiges of a one-time lay ministry) or other distinctive practices. They have even less guidance in formulating new procedures for new times, except what may be uncritically absorbed from the culture.

It is probably accurate to say that among the "cooperative" Disciples the formula has really become FU. Some of them have violently repudiated the element of restoration, a small group tried to alchemize it into something it never was (e.g., "restoring the spirit of the New Testament"), while the majority neither realize that it is gone nor miss it—even on occasion repeating the word with a reflex of traditional emotion.

F. Freedom remains a prime value among Disciples. Most of them recognize that the adjective "Christian" sets certain limits on liberty; some would like to see the limits clarified but are not sure how this can be done. Meanwhile, the organized brotherhood has countered a tendency toward anarchy by developing a conscience on responsible cooperation. Disciples have reared an impressive structure of awkwardly intermeshed but genuinely effective voluntary agencies which report to the International (U.S.A. and Canada) Convention of Christian Churches (Disciples of Christ). In effect, they have a central budget. With no theologically legitimized structure of authority or coercion, the enterprise succeeds through conscientious commitment, effective communication (even propaganda) and—as any realist must admit—the knowledge that a minister is more likely to get ahead if he works within the cooperative machinery. Disciples continue to resist any restriction on freedom. Many of them will also resist any change in the particular institutions by which Disciples have sought to protect their liberty, under the illusion that other American Christians are not so fully dedicated to this ideal.

U. Unity moved to the emotional fore with each passing decade during the first half of the 20th century. During the past generation the International Convention authorized unity negotiations with the American Baptist Convention and with the Conference on Church Union (Greenwich Plan); both terminated without success. The Unity Commission is now engaged in conversations with the United Church of Christ and with the Consultation on Church Union (the so-called Blake-Pike proposal). But despite a vast reservoir of commitment to a united church (outlines not defined), there is genuine disillusionment with shining ideals gone glimmering, disillusionment accompanied by the suspicion that the goal of a united church may be as illusory as that of world peace or prohibition.

III

Disciples have dubbed their great "program emphasis" for the 1960s the Decade of Decision. This decade, and perhaps the next, may well prove to be just that—a period when they must wrestle with decisions affecting their destiny. I would suggest four areas of concern.

1. *The nature of the church.* The old-line Disciples had a biblically determined if wooden doctrine of the church which was basically sound except for its failure to discern the need for corporate institutions beyond the congregation. With the collapse of restorationist legalism went a general de-emphasis on the biblical doctrine of the church. The professional ministry, the prevailing scheme of congregational organization, the omnipresence of church program—all emerged as pragmatic considerations: "so that the church can get the job done," with "success" measured in statistical terms. Sermons are no longer very doctrinal, nor necessarily biblical. The present generation seems scarcely to know what the church is—and there is no creed, no liturgy, no presbytery or episcopate, no popular knowledge of the Bible to provide direction. A "great people" must come again to understand the nature and calling of the church.

2. *A guiding principle.* The crucial issue, many Disciples would say, is that of authority. Though absolute directives—such as the old restorationist dogma was thought to provide—are not to be found, the church still needs guidance.

In keeping with the best in their tradition, Disciples can find sufficient guidance in an *ecumenically responsible biblical theology corporately applied to the church's present mission.* Detailed formulations of answers to current problems must come out of spiritual and intellectual labor; we have neither an infallible absolute to guide us in all particulars nor a void which leaves us without direction. But in line with the principles here advocated, with full openness to the insights of our fellow Christians, including the most responsible scholarship, we can expose mind and heart in all seriousness to the biblical witness. We can ponder the scriptural testimony both to the great event of Jesus Christ and to the meaning which the apostolic church found in it, both to the gospel which the early church proclaimed and to the church which was created and shaped by that gospel. We can theologize about that witness, reflecting on it as modern men, letting the living Lord of the church speak to us, as by the power of the Holy Spirit the biblical witness addresses us in our condition. We can take counsel together as to the means by which we in our time can fulfill the imperative laid upon the church by that gospel.

Here is authentically Christian guidance for the church, especially for a communion without authoritative structure, accepted creed or long tradition. Some who rebelled against a fundamentalist restorationism will perhaps be slow to come to acceptance of even this much authority—but can anything less be authentically Christian? Many will wish for more detailed guidance from an infallible source—but is it not the lesson of history that such guidance is not available? The church must live by faith. If W is taken for witness, WFU may prove a much more stable compound than RFU. Disciples may still find meaningful guidance in the witness of the Scripture to the living Lord and the serving church.

3. *A structure of brotherhood.* Out of the strong sense of mission which has characterized the movement, a congeries of institutions for fellowship and common action emerged as mass (not delegate) conventions and independent societies, with no ecclesiastical character or status. Legally autonomous and ostensibly secular corporations, more than 70 such agencies (including colleges and state organizations) now share in the general missionary and benevolent budget raised by "unified promotion." Relationships among these bodies have become incredibly complicated.

In 1961 the International Convention appointed some 120 representative Disciples to serve as a Commission on Brotherhood Restructure. It is seeking to clarify relationships and responsibilities among the agencies and planning bodies, as well as to outline a more responsible relationship among congregations, the state conventions and the International Convention. It may undertake much more; it may achieve much less.

Some Disciples see in the restructure movement—the most talked-about issue in the brotherhood today—occasion for a thoroughgoing reconsideration of the nature of the church and an earnest search for renewal; others foresee the imposition of a massive new ecclesiasticism. Given the nature of Disciples, the prophecies of the latter show little likelihood of proving true, but the hopes of the former may indeed come to pass. There is a strong possibility that in the next decade cooperative Disciples will move to a more coherent form of congregational polity, retaining the high sense of local responsibility which has characterized their churches at their best, but linking them together with an avowedly churchly structure more suited to the Christian mission in our time and better calculated to express the corporate nature of the church.

There have been some minor efforts to deal with the schism-that-is-not-yet-a-schism; for instance, several locally initiated "conferences on internal unity" have been held. But it is not likely that the "independent" ranks, still ardently restorationist, are about to embrace the principles of brotherhood cooperation and of ecumenical involvement, nor, on the other hand, that the main body of cooperative Disciples will allow the structure of cooperation to be vitiated.

4. *The obligation to union.* Gradually Disciples have come to realize that Christian union will not be achieved along the lines envisioned by the early fathers. The sectarianism of the middle period attracts only a dwindling following today. So Disciples are left with a powerful tradition, enforced by the newer ecumenical climate, impelling them to do something about Christian unity; but they lack a common mind as to what should be done. True, they have already done a great deal. They have given loyal support to councils of churches. The United Christian Missionary Society has gained general acceptance for its "strategy of world

mission," which repudiates sectarian motivation and renounces
the denominational approach to the task. The freedom of the
missions to find their places within the emerging united churches
has been affirmed with the assurance of continuing support from
the society. If "Disciples" in the Philippines, Japan, Thailand and
other lands can find their way into united churches, what about
the "pioneers of Christian unity" in the United States?

For nearly twenty years conversations with the Congregationalists have been in the offing. Since the United Church of Christ
came into being two meetings have been held, and members of
the United Church and Disciples unity commissions have grown
in mutual understanding and appreciation. No insuperable barriers
have been discovered. If the commissions should be given a mandate by their denominations to devise a plan of union, there is
every reason to believe that they could do so.

Shortly before the first joint meeting of the two commissions
the "Blake-Pike" proposal for a major four-way union (Episcopal,
Presbyterian, Methodist, United) was dramatically thrust upon
the consideration of American Protestants. Sponsored by the
United Church, Disciples have been invited into the Consultation
on Church Union (which now includes the Evangelical United
Brethren as well) which stemmed from that proposal. It is fair
to say that Disciples went to the Oberlin meeting of the consultation somewhat skeptical and came away genuinely excited as to
the possibility, by the grace of God, that a major union could
be achieved.

The difficulties over any union loom large. They tend to be
verbalized by Disciples in the form of "problems to be resolved"
—problems having to do with baptism, weekly communion, the
place of creeds, church government, the process of approving
and consummating any union. In essence, these problems are not
insuperable obstacles in themselves; they are rather evidence of a
widespread indifference to the work of union. Such indifference
seems traceable to the fact that all ministers already have their
hands more than full with present problems, or to the lack of

opportunity most Disciples have had for the kind of meaningful
ecumenical experience which brings a profound sense of spiritual
and theological oneness with other Christians and a profound
sense of the sinfulness and meaninglessness of continued separation.

IV

From the old RFU formula, R is gone. If the sinister lethargy
about union efforts which now tempts many Disciples should prevail, U could drop out also—and what would be the meaning
of a self-satisfied denomination committed only to freedom? If
Disciples should revise their formula to the WFU suggested above,
they might well find themselves no longer a separate and hesitant
people but a vital part of an emerging church—ecumenical, free,
ready for meaningful mission to the 20th century.

As a grateful and committed Disciple, I am convinced that the
breakdown of our old structures and of our old self-assurance is
not a cause for dismay but the gracious work of God. He has
used our separate witness—and that of many others—more glori-
ously than can be explained by the inherent power of anything
in it. But that day is gone. And it is not enough to breathe "spiritual" unity while still pursuing our separate ways. Now God is
leading his church to discover the true source of its oneness in
his reconciling work—not for the church's sake, but for the
world's. For if he can truly imbue the church with a sense of
wonder at his unfettered grace which breaks down the structures
of our long separation and heals us with renewing wholeness, may
he not be preparing us to carry his witness to a world which
scarcely hears the gospel as it is mumbled by separate and self-
satisfied denominations?

Surely Disciples must continue the hard intellectual work of
the theological renaissance in which we are now engaged so that
we may discern more clearly the nature of the church and the
principles by which it is guided; surely we must provide effective,
rational, churchly structure for carrying out our mission. But

this is not enough. The irony would be too great should we ever
rest as a theologically mature, organizationally effective denomination perpetuating "a great American religious tradition." God is
even now seeking to renew his church with one heart and a new
spirit. If we let him do his work in us and if we obediently do our
work for him, he will give to us and to many of the brethren from
whom we are now separate a greater witness than the witness
of the Disciples alone, and a larger destiny than any of us has
yet dreamed.

10. UNITED PRESBYTERIANS: PROPHECY VS. TRADITION

John R. Fry*

Among members of the United Presbyterian Church in the U.S.A.
the new theology of the laity, compounded of New Testament
exegesis, Bonhoeffer, World Council study documents, ecumenical
conference language, and a rough, from-the-hip contextualist
ethics, has caught hold—as much as and perhaps more than in
any other American Protestant denomination. Not all 3.2 million
United Presbyterians are prepared to define the "servanthood of
the laity" as the "true Christian ministry," or to do away with
religion (following the strictures of Bonhoeffer), or to eliminate
clergy-only ordination, or to begin daring ecumenical ventures.
But a significant number of the denomination's leaders—both
clergy and lay—have adopted what for want of a better word I
shall call, taking my cue from the World Council-sponsored
ecumenical institute near Geneva, the "Bossey" point of view.
Parish ministers, university pastors, board secretaries, theologically

* Mr. Fry is news editor for *Presbyterian Life* magazine.

sophisticated laymen in surprising numbers have adopted an openness to the world as a place in which ministry is to be performed,
rather than a region to be converted and made part of the church.

Except for the theologically "in" laymen, the leaders we are
referring to here are very much occupied with the religion they
ideologically despise and are supported to a dramatic extent by
the suburban cult churches they so regularly fulminate against.
The tension-producing presence of "Bossey" theology in the
midst of numerous Presbyterians who are more traditionally pious
and status-quo-oriented is astonishing and may even provoke some
major changes in denominational structure and stance.

I

Item: At the Des Moines General Assembly in May the United
Presbyterian denomination finally, after years of talking, put
$500,000 into a Commission on Religion and Race and sent to the
presbyteries for approval a proposed constitutional amendment
that would prohibit racial discrimination in the acceptance of
members by particular congregations. The young and middle-
aged "turks" responsible for getting these minimal actions before
the Assembly were exultant when the Assembly voted affirm-
atively on them. Well they might have been. It was a significant
and overdue pair of acts.

Of course, $500,000 worth of fancy witnessing, demonstration
and the like is not going to do very much to alter the shape of
the desegregation now proceeding apace—not even if the whole
sum were spent for picket signs. What would really amount to
something would be for a majority of the bucolic, heartland Presbyterians to enter solemnly into open-occupancy covenants, especially in the largest metropolitan suburbs. If only 1,000 of the
United Presbyterians who will sell their suburban houses in the
next year were to give preference to Negro buyers, the impact
would be greater than that of a Commission on Religion and Race
that spent $10 million during the same year.

Here is an instance of the tension between the denominational provocateurs and the great inertia-bound majority of Presbyterians who currently are, according to the polls, seriously appraising Senator Barry Goldwater as a presidential possibility. No matter how much the awakened leaders want to act and speak for it, the denomination must take into consideration the wishes of its 9,000 churches.

Item: At the same General Assembly a church-state report was adopted which anticipated the Supreme Court decision on Bible reading and prayer in public schools and which in general sought to clarify church-state relationships in America. This document exhibits considerable theological vitality and is unmistakably "Bossey" in spirit and content. But although provincial opposition to the report was strenuous, it was adopted—a remarkably clear victory of common sense and biblical sense over the uninformed chauvinism of the heartland. The mere fact that such an advanced theological point of view could get a fair hearing shows the extent of denominationwide acceptance of the new theology. The report's *adoption* demonstrates the fact the denomination can change point of view and structure under the pressure of the new theology.

What's ahead for the United Presbyterians will be determined largely by how the issue between the denomination's "Bossey" hotshots, its traditional leaders and its members in the heartland turns out. One might hedge his bets by considering the essence of all Parkinsonian laws, namely, that corporate bodies tend to shift from foot to foot in inverse ratio to the amount of constructive remodeling that needs to be done. But that is a coward's way out, and probably the cynical hedger would lose his bets; there are likely to be some notable changes in the denomination, one way or another.

II

For one thing, an unprecedented capital funds campaign stands in the wings of denominational history. The raising of the huge sum of $100 million is not exactly the same old pedestrian business of ecclesiastical upholstery that is so characteristic of American Christians. It is, for reasons I will elaborate, a fateful occurrence for the denomination.

The funds to be raised are projected for use in building up seminaries, denominationally related colleges, overseas educational institutions, new church development projects, metropolitan ministries. The boards responsible for the on-going administration of these institutions and programs do not have sufficient funds in their annual budgets to provide the necessary new and replacement facilities. The annual "general mission" giving is not enough to take care of such needs (even though the per capita giving of United Presbyterians is second only to the Southern Baptists among major denominations). Moreover, of late the national boards have initiated increasing numbers of special programs, special ministries and so on.

In asking for $100 million the boards and agencies are asking not only for a vote of confidence but also for approval of the expansionist activities that have made the campaign necessary. The issue can be put in this way: Are we United Presbyterians going to have a church which is controlled—or served—chiefly by national boards? Or are we going to take care of capital needs locally and let the national boards carry out nationally oriented programs on a modest budget? That is the way the issue looks— and it looks like a lively one, too. A proposal presented to the Des Moines General Assembly and now being circulated among the presbyteries for concurrence or nonconcurrence calls for the establishment of regional synods, its intention being to counter the kind of centralization that has been taking place at a brisk pace since the end of World War II.

Will grass-roots dissatisfaction with national boards and bureaucracy in general, coupled with a yearning for closer local control of colleges, seminaries, national missions projects and general-mission fund campaigns, be so keenly and concertedly felt that the capital funds campaign will turn out to be an ignominious bust? Or will the United Presbyterians come through with all that money and give the boards the funds to carry out the kind of job that Jesus Christ commands? It is a big question, and to a real extent the future of the denomination depends on how rank-and-file members answer.

The capital funds issue reveals a yet deeper dilemma within the ranks of United Presbyterians—that of institutionalism. The denomination's institutional officials are about as sophisticated as officials can get. They are, believe it or not, anti-institutional in their own personal ideology. In intimate conversation they confess that they want to "infiltrate" the institution, or, in some cases, to "destroy" the institution—but from the inside. Few of them see themselves as happy workers within the institutional vineyard. Most of them talk, think and dream about getting out—but they remain.

Of course, the uneasiness that goes with such a mood is institutionally healthy. The officials are never satisfied, are always a shade hostile or on edge, are always trying to get reform—or a compromise, on the ground that half a reform is better than the status quo. These officials are the same people, mind you, who are going to spend that $100 million, if and when it comes in. Such an eventuality would have double-edged consequences. Inevitably the officials are going to strengthen the institution they feign to deplore. Inevitably they will develop ever greater concentrations of power and become more and more a national staff running a national church. But the other consequence needs clarification also. The very people who are most hesitant to further the movement toward centralization are the ones best equipped—because most sanguine—to be in the driver's seat. If we are going to have an ever more powerful bureaucracy, we are fortunate to have so many people of "Bossey" orientation to run it.

III

The distinctive mark of American Presbyterianism—that which differentiates it from Reformed polity in other parts of the world

—is the uniquely powerful role of the presbytery. Recent decisions by the General Assembly's permanent judicial commission have underlined that power. Presbyteries, accordingly, need not become mere administrative arms of national boards which, theoretically, serve rather than dominate the church. Presbyteries have the power to repudiate any program produced in Philadelphia or New York city. They have the power, at General Assembly, to issue mandates that change the programs, projects, plans, procedures, budgets—and mistakes—of the national boards and agencies. They can also refuse to go along with a General Assembly capital funds campaign.

The other side of the dilemma appears when a loosely confederated string of presbyteries, each one powerful in its own right, tries, in conjunction with an "underprivileged" national staff, to be a United Presbyterian Church *in the U.S.A.* Can the presbyteries of New York or Chicago or Los Angeles run a full-swing inner city program, support area colleges and seminaries, provide curriculum for church schools, maintain an imaginative overseas ecumenical witness, and, with other presbyteries, ensure real theological and ecclesiastical continuity? And if the strong, rich, well organized presbyteries would have to answer a realistic No to that question, what would the smaller, poorer, weaker presbyteries answer? Action by the individual, the local church, the presbytery is not sufficient; today action must be on a national scale to be strong enough to be anything. And there is the dilemma.

One has only to recall the impact of the wire photos showing the denomination's stated clerk, Eugene Carson Blake, being arrested for participating in a demonstration against racial segregation in Baltimore to recognize the power of a strong national church organization that can act responsibly under the mandate of all its affiliated churches. In such a church the power is concentrated and ready to be used. Fortuitously, the United Presbyterian bureaucracy is about as well equipped as any bureaucracy imaginable to handle the money—and the centralization that goes with it—envisioned in the capital funds campaign.

During 1962-3 a nationwide series of meetings on the nature of the ministry was held, for the ordained on week days and for the unordained on weekends. While still not fully evaluated, these meetings revealed that the unordained are more willing to consider radically anti-institutional measures and Bossey-type thinking than are the ordained. The laymen regularly scorched the pretty paint right off the walls of the national organization, while the clergy groups were plainly reluctant to countenance the idea of a church in which, for instance, "ordination to service" would be viewed as occurring at baptism (thus doing away with clergy ordination and the traditional clergy altogether). These seminars provided two clues as to what's ahead for the capital funds drive: the laymen are restively suspicious about institutional bureaucracy; the clergy are defensively protective concerning a strong institution and a strong "union."

Let us think about new church development briefly, in order to assess what it portends for the Presbyterian future. At the same time that Bossey-type prophets are summoning up testimony concerning the inadequacy of the traditional parish model "church" to which Christians "go" for worship, recreation and study—and to whose altar Christians are supposed to bring the world—presbyteries and synods, in cooperation with and financed by the Board of National Missions, are putting up such churches as fast as they can get funds. The developers constitute an offense to the prophets, and vice versa. In the view of the developers, the way to be a strong denomination is to build new churches, get more members, put more money in the central receiving agency's till, and, eventually, perform more witness in American communities. The prophets contend that to spend precious funds on a lot of new buildings and hardware is not only criminally wasteful but theologically sinful, perpetuating the same old ineffectual individualistic pietism that has been characteristic of American Protestantism for a century.

Clear though the issue may be, the United Presbyterians are not likely to break away from the Protestant pattern at *this* point. When it comes to competing for church sites in a high-potential area, you may count on the United Presbyterians to be there, checkbook in one hand and comity agreement in the other. Had they listened to the prophets they would not have understood a word, so tied are they to their notion of what it is that Presbyterians do: they build churches to get new members to get more money to build new churches to get . . .

IV

Finally, ecumenicity is ahead for all of us Protestants. United Presbyterians are participants in merger talks with the Episcopal and Methodist churches, the United Church of Christ and others. Regardless of how it is spelled or how the good Bishop Pike gets into the title of the proposal, it is still spelled Blake and it still dominates the ecumenical horizon. Dr. Blake, after a rousing General Assembly vote of confidence in Buffalo in regard to entering into merger talks, has good reason to feel that United Presbyterians will go further than any other mainline group down the road to unity.

All Protestant denominations are coming to see, I should hope, that regardless of how intensely interesting internal church affairs are to church people, they are not interesting and are often barely credible to the unchurched. There may be a degree of struggle going on within every denomination, as there is in ours, to break the ironclad identification of the Protestant church with the middle class and its polished bourgeois ethos. But it is a pathetic struggle of a few against astronomical odds. Surely it has become clear that our time for speaking and acting in the racial crisis has passed. We may wave a few signs—but denominational image-sharpening vies with the glory of God as principal motivation.

The point is not that the Protestant churches, including our own, are irrelevant. The situation is infinitely worse than that. We have been fighting on the wrong side of every major political, social and economic issue for so long that no one gives us credit for our last-minute switches to the right (i.e., the winning) side. The point seems to be that we have countenanced and sanctioned injustice for so long that to the oppressed we seem to be among the oppressors. If they are right—and they ought to know—then what's ahead for American Protestantism *and* the United Presbyterians had better be reckoned along eschatological lines that anticipate . . . lightning.

11. MORMONISM ON THE MOVE

Roy A. Cheville*

Many of us Latter Day Saints are concerned about where we are going today and tomorrow. We may differ as to what the main questions are and what the answers would be, but we are at one in being concerned. We realize that mere carrying on will not be enough.

At the outset it must be recognized that there is considerable variation among the several bodies that have come out of the Latter Day Saint movement. There are differences in theology, in church administration, in materials and methods. No blanket answer is possible. Add to these the natural and healthy differences among the members of each group and the picture becomes quite complicated.

1

The Latter Day Saint movement had its origin in western New York in the decade 1820-30. The Church of Jesus Christ of Lat-

* Mr. Cheville is presiding evangelist of the Reorganized Church of Jesus Christ of Latter Day Saints, with headquarters in Independence, Missouri.

ter-day Saints was organized in 1830 under pioneer prophet Joseph Smith, Jr. Smith was killed in Illinois in 1844. The headquarters community of the movement was then in the Illinois town of Nauvoo.

With Smith's death divisions began. Led by Brigham Young, president of the church's "twelve apostles," a large body of the Saints left Nauvoo in 1846 and migrated westward. By 1847 they were beginning to settle in the Salt Lake region of what is now Utah. This body, officially designated the "Church of Jesus Christ of Latter-day Saints" but popularly called "Mormons," is today the largest in the whole movement, numbering well over a million members.

Some of the Nauvoo Saints, however, did not go with the Brigham Young group. In 1853 a number of those who had stayed behind set up the "Reorganized Church of Jesus Christ of Latter Day Saints." In 1860 Joseph Smith III, the son of the founder, became their prophet-president. This body now centers in Independence, Missouri. As was to be expected, there have been strains and disputes aplenty between the "Brighamites" centering in Salt Lake City and the "Josephites" centering in Independence.

During these decades of confusion several smaller bodies came into existence—for example, the Church of Christ (Hedrickites), which has possession of the central area of the land called the "temple lot" in Independence. Each of these small groups considers itself the true successor of the original movement.

The "Utah Church" and the "Reorganized Church" are the two groups considered in this article. Both hold to some basics but differ as to how these are to be interpreted and applied. Thus for each church we need to inquire not only *what* is believed but also *how* it is believed. Broadly speaking, these fundamentals are held in common: (1) belief in the decline of Christianity through the centuries and the consequent necessity for "restoration" of the gospel and the spiritual dynamic of early Christianity; (2) the prophetic calling of Joseph Smith and others in effecting this "restoration"; (3) the constant renewal of ministerial author-

ity through continuing revelation; (4) the centrality of Jesus
Christ in this revelatory experience; (5) re-establishment of the
church of Jesus Christ pictured in the New Testament, with the
polity and spiritual dynamic and the rites and sacraments described there; (6) the present-tense spiritual fellowship of saints,
centering in a community known as Zion; (7) multiple canons of
scripture, including the Bible of the Hebrews and the early Christians, the *Book of Mormon* and various contributions made in
later and present times.

II

Let us consider the "Utah Church" first. In its various periodicals—notably the *Improvement Era*, which is described as "The
Voice of the Church" and every month carries a section titled
"The Church Moves On"—it sets forth what it considers its
major news. On the basis of these publications the following may
be identified as the church's major concerns: (1) appointments to
administrative positions; (2) statistics of membership; (3) con-
truction and dedication of church buildings; (4) construction
of and activities in the temples in which rituals pertain
more specifically to the hereafter; (5) genealogical studies
pertaining to baptismal rites in the temple for the deceased; (6)
missionary operations, especially of the many youths serving on
a two-year self-supporting basis; (7) organization of new "stakes"
(the Mormon term for jurisdictional units); (8) the semi-annual
general conference; (9) the priesthood program with advance-
ment from office to office; (10) church institutions for higher
education; (11) family life which is to begin in the temple with
marriage "for eternity"; (12) youth activities that are expressional,
social, recreational.

It is safe to predict that in the years ahead the church will continue to pursue the objectives and policies thus revealed. There
is an atmosphere of confidence in this body. It may be expected
to extend and intensify proselyting activities at home and abroad,

making use of all media of communication; to involve all members in the church's activities; to provide social welfare facilities for its people; and in general to do everything possible to foster a living sense of the heritage of the movement.

III

Like every other religious institution today, however, the Utah Church faces critical problems, some of which so far have scarcely been formulated by its leaders and have altogether escaped the notice of the average member. Perhaps the most acute of these problems arises from the fact that Mormons are necessarily moving more and more into social and intellectual contacts with the world at large (incidentally, the church's rate of numerical growth is greater outside its central area, namely Utah and adjacent states). Under such circumstances control of theological thinking will not be easy. How interpret the Mormon gospel or Mormon temple practices to persons of critical spirit and intellectual breadth? How perpetuate Mormon views of family life and marriage for eternity against the impact of modern society? On the organizational side there is the problem of maintaining cohesion in a church located in many lands, a church moreover that has a distinctly American flavor. And of special concern just now is the question of the place of the Negro in Mormonism.

To cope successfully with these and other problems of the times the Utah Church relies heavily on its time-honored resources: its centralized administration and the authoritarian voice of its presidents, apostles and bishops; the appeal and holding power of the temple service with promise of good estate in the hereafter; the tradition of Mormon pioneering; the two-year missionary service of youth; the reverence of Joseph Smith as prophet; the publicity program that builds up the feeling of a growing church. Can these means speak effectively and meaningfully in the days ahead? Can they hold Mormons and appeal to non-Mormons? Will the

Mormonism that flourished from 1847 until a decade or so ago be able to hold its own after 1963? By what criteria will future leaders of the church be able to declare that "the church moves on"?

The Reorganized Church of Latter Day Saints has had a different experience. While the Utah church was geographically concentrated for decades, the Reorganized Church has always lived among non-Mormons. Only recently has there been a concentration of members in and around Independence, Missouri, and even there they are not a majority. In other words, these Reorganized members have had to learn to live in a social environment which at first they felt to be hostile. Over the years, however, they have come into easier relations with non-Saints. It is a significant day in a group's life when it attains a measure of accommodation to the surrounding social world. This development means that the group's sense of unity will not be achieved through persecution and external compulsion, but must come through internal cohesive forces. The Reorganized Church must stand for enough that is distinctive and must cultivate this distinctiveness so as to foster morale and pride in belonging.

A church that grows at all will have some growing pains. Generally a group that begins in conflict with prevailing religious groups comes to be concerned with respectability, hence will develop institutionally. But while gaining social standing it may lose its own soul. Conscientious Latter Day Saints are aware of this danger.

IV

Today the Independence church is experiencing strains of no little consequence. It finds itself in a situation of crisis. This is no cause for lamentation, for spiritual strides forward generally come precisely in times when a group must decide which way to go. The Reorganized Church faces two major questions: (1) the relationship of administrative groups in conducting its affairs, together with the operation of hierarchical and democratic aspects of ecclesiastical government; and (2) identification of basic Latter Day Saint theology. The church believes that its own organic structure affects the lives of members. It makes a difference whether the members actively share in carrying on the affairs of the body ecclesiastical or whether they only assent to decisions taken by the few. The church is described as a theocratic democracy or a democratic theocracy. How bring the two aspects to work together?

Equally difficult is the question of Reorganized theology. Certainly the church has a right to exist only as it has something distinctive to contribute to the spiritual life of the world. Otherwise, keen-thinking members would say, it might as well haul down its flag. But what are the distinctives? And what is their meaning and significance for our times? I venture to name certain basics that have to be lived and thought through.

Vital to the whole Mormon movement is a concept of the role of the ever-living Christ in the process of salvation. The initial experience of Joseph Smith in 1820 was Christ-centered. The Mormon pioneers believed that a person could meet this ever-living Christ in whatever today he happened to live in, for the revelation of Jesus Christ is more than an event in history. How can this encounter be as vital in the 1960s as it was for the early Saints?

Another vital concept concerns the nature and functions of the Holy Spirit. The spirit, Latter Day Saints believe, has always been at the heart of their movement. If this faith drops out of the movement, its dynamic will go. But how express this faith today? In this matter the Reorganized Church is going through some of the growing pains that Paul perceived in the Corinthian congregation. Some are hungry for easily discernible manifestations. Others would lift the people's qualifications and level of desire so that experience of the Holy Spirit will carry edification and enlightenment.

V

A third important Mormon principle has to do with the purpose and process of Zion. From the beginning all Reorganized bodies of Latter Day Saints have believed in the setting up of a saintly community called Zion, with Independence, Missouri, as the "center place." But there are wide differences in their views as to the motivation, method, manpower and mission of Zion. Many think of it as a place of refuge for the Saints as ills of the world increase; others consider it essential in God's program of ministering to the world, a spiritual nucleus in spreading the gospel to the world. Thus there are differences in conceptions of apartness from the world, of utilization of human resources, of expectancy of marvelous manifestations. The identification of Zion is of tremendous import. It involves the church's own self-identification.

The message and method of evangelism constitute a fourth important problem. All Reorganized members look upon evangelism as inherent in the movement. Today concerned ministers are saying that the church urgently needs a fresh, creative approach to evangelism; that the way of a "packaged" gospel, of argumentation and debate, of running down other churches is not going to be effective, for it is at variance with the spirit of the gospel. The Saints must live with and love those to whom they are going to carry God's message. It would be disastrous, however, were the church to water down the message in order to make it easily understood. Related to this is the problem of the purposes and procedures in world mission. What are we setting out to do in Japan, in French Polynesia, in Germany? What is our Christian motivation for going? How do we speak to cultures that differ from our own?

A fifth pressing concern is the function of prophetic inspiration and the expression of prophetic ministry. The concept of revelation as always contemporary is a cardinal point of faith among Latter Day Saints. We believe that the structure of the church provides for the prophetic office. Some think that prayer and fasting in order that God may speak are the major requisites for prophetic ministry. Others, while calling for the spiritual fitness that comes through such disciplines, emphasize the need for personal and general development to bring about capacity and sensitivity so God can speak significantly. These see inspiration functioning in the many fields of enlightened living. On the ascendancy of one or the other of these views much of the future of the church depends.

Finally, there is the problem of the interpretation of the rise of the Latter Day Saint movement and of the scriptures that emerged out of it. How shall the *Book of Mormon* and the *Doctrine and Covenants* be approached? Shall they be critically analyzed? Some members would discount all such exploration; others would study the language, content and emergence of these documents. Some declare that validation of the *Book of Mormon* must come from the book itself. These hold up as the chief message of the book the affirmation of the universal Christ who manifested himself on the western continent. Thus today it is not enough to ask "Do you believe in the *Book of Mormon?*" One must ask also "*How* do you believe in it?"

VI

What is ahead for the Latter Day Saints? The question cannot be evaded or dismissed. No church today can "carry on as usual." Each has to consider what it has that is sound, God-inspired and essential to man's salvation, here and hereafter. Speaking as a member of the Reorganized Church of Jesus Christ of Latter Day Saints, I think of it as a creative, consecrated minority in a great, great world. If it seems preposterous to think of a group of a few thousand as having any place among more than three billion, recall the dynamic power of a company of twelve two thousand years ago. But smallness and fervor alone are not enough. What is needed is a clear reading of the times, a prophetic sense of mission and message, and a strongly witnessing fellowship.

This is a critical time for the whole Mormon movement, a time

that calls for vision and verve. And what a time! One feels like
repeating the prayer of the eight-year-old boy who was about
to take part in a children's pageant: "Now, God, help us so we
won't flub in this!" With God's help, we shall have communion
and commission for today and the coming day.

12. AMERICA'S CATHOLIC COMMUNITY: INCREASING INVOLVEMENT

Bernard Cooke, S.J.*

Charismatically gifted, the prophets of Israel could stand in their
moment of history and, in the light of their people's past, see the
deeper orientations of history as it promised to unfold. For the
Christian of today, without such prophetic grace, to foretell the
future workings of the Spirit in the church would be folly. And
it would be even worse folly for a Roman Catholic theologian
to essay to predict what lies ahead for his church at the very moment when his church is engaged in a worldwide council whose
objective is to examine the deepest currents of faith and religious
life. Yet the important developments which mark the present state
of Catholic thought and life provide some guideposts for a judgment as to where the next few decades will lead Catholics in the
pursuit of their faith.

I

For approximately three decades now, and with accelerating
pace, modern biblical scholarship has had a major influence on

* Father Cooke is chairman of the department of theology at Marquette
University, Milwaukee, Wisconsin.

Catholic theology. There is no reason for expecting that this influence will not continue. As a matter of fact, just the opposite is to be anticipated, for there exists a considerable body of scientific clarification of Scripture that has not yet been brought to bear on Catholic theologizing. Moreover, the detailed and painstaking efforts of scholarship in the areas of history, linguistics and archaeology are culminating in serious studies in biblical theology and hermeneutics. As this growing biblical theologizing has its impact on Catholic dogmatics, there cannot but be an important effect of clarification and purification. Already this influence has modified the standard "manual method" in Catholic theological instruction: the Bible is less and less considered a thesaurus of apt texts to bolster scholastic formulations of faith; it is gradually coming into its own as a source and guide for the deepening of faith and understanding.

Allied with this biblical influence, though not identical with it, is the increased influence of studies in historiography and in the contemporary historical mentality. Evolving very largely along structural lines, aware of the facts of history but never really introducing the historical dimension of the truth of faith into its point of view, classical scholastic theology found itself out of touch with much that is deepest in the modern intellectual world. The past few years, however, have seen a most noteworthy change in this regard. Not only has there been a wealth of monographs investigating the actual historical situation of the faith-events and of the developing formulations of this faith; there has also been an increasing theological awareness that the very historical nature of these faith-events must be an integral part of theology's object. This view has had an effect on all areas of Catholic theology, perhaps most significantly on the resurgence of sacramental theology and on the notion of the church as the continuator and bearer of *Heilsgeschichte*, "history of salvation." Important as these developments are, they are yet in their infancy, and can be expected to have even greater impact in the immediate future. Not that the valid aspects of scholastic developments will be abandoned;

for it is a characteristic of the Catholic theological growth that it absorbs into the new the perennially valuable contribution of past thought.

Another important phenomenon of contemporary Catholic thought is the confrontation with the "personalist" strains of present-day thinking. Theologians like Jean Mouroux and Hans Urs von Balthasar exemplify this absorption into the Catholic theological synthesis of the person-centered thought that one associates with modern psychology and existentialism. This influence has very profoundly coincided with the concrete and personal thought which has flowed into theology from its awakened encounter with the Bible. Thus far, this personalist influence has only begun to touch the major areas of Catholic theologizing; but one can expect to see it exerting considerable influence in the years ahead in dogmatic discussions of grace and Christology as well as in moral and spiritual theology. As this happens, one can anticipate a resultant shift in the content and tone of catechetical instruction and preaching in Catholic circles; there, too, the tendency to approach faith-understanding from the point of view of the person—already noticeable—should become more marked.

Deriving from this personalist interest and from studies of the Scriptures is the attention paid by Catholic theologians to what one might call the "communication aspects" of Christianity. Deepening understanding of the complexity of revelation, of biblical inspiration, of tradition and faith, has resulted in a re-examination of the entire process of faith. This re-examination involves to some extent breaking away from the problematics inherited from Reformation and Counter-Reformation times. One very interesting and promising stream of thought in this area is the development of a "theology of the Word," a theology that cuts through the previous categorizings of Christology, revelation, sacraments, ecclesiology. For the moment, this emphasis on the evangelical elements in Christianity is still somewhat limited to theologians like Karl Rahner, to those influenced by the so-called "kerygmatic theology." However, it seems quite safe to say that this area of investigation has solidly established itself in Catholic theological circles, and that it will have important repercussions on the entire theory and practice of Catholic religious formation. Obviously, too, it will form an important bridge of understanding with those currents of Protestant thought that have traditionally emphasized the role of the inspired word of God.

Perhaps the area of Catholic theology that will develop most significantly in the next couple of decades is that of study of the sacraments, for it is there that all the influences mentioned above come to focus. Such theological investigation, already launched in an important way, is part and parcel of the contemporary interest in symbolism; as a matter of fact, the discussion of symbol and its role in society, language, art, psychology, has contributed insights of considerable value to Catholic theologizing about sacraments. Sacraments, of course, have always been a standard element in Catholic theology and life; but what is coming to pass now is a more profound insight into transformation of the person, into the role of faith-commitment in sacrament, into the ability of sacrament to integrate the person within himself and with the world of persons in which he is situated. Since sacramental theology is ultimately inseparable from ecclesiology, emphasis on these actions of the Christian community will inevitably lead to greater appreciation of the dynamic reality of the church, to greater realization of the church's role in history. It is clear that this development will link sacramental theology with contemporary investigation into what is termed "theology of culture," and so will involve Catholic theology very deeply in the question of the humanistic pertinence of Christianity.

Anyone familiar with the World Council of Churches knows how the topic of the church has dominated the discussions of this group for the past few decades. Even though there has been careful study and rather anguished appraisal of the nature and the function of the church, the Christian communities participating in the WCC are still far from agreement as to the nature and function of the church. To quite an extent something comparable has been happening in Roman Catholic theological circles. If anyone was unaware of this movement in Catholic ecclesiology, the Second Vatican Council made the fact evident: a clear majority of the bishops present at the Council's first session expressed their dissatisfaction with the schema on the church as presented by the Council's theological commission.

This reaction of the Council Fathers reflected a change in viewpoint which has been slowly gaining ground since the middle of the 19th century. Some theologians and churchmen have felt an uneasiness with a too "structural" understanding of the church, and have been painstakingly complementing this view by consideration of the church as the Body of Christ, as the community of faith. Biblical studies, too, have drawn attention to the scriptural ideas of the church: the new Israel, the people of God, the bride of Christ. In the decree on the liturgy which has already appeared, the bishops of the Second Vatican Council have indicated their preference for describing the church in these more biblical terms.

This tendency would seem to indicate, both in the case of Catholic theology and in the more widespread understanding of the Catholic faithful, that an increased appreciation of the church as mystery will offset the previous emphasis on the external organizational aspects. Christ's role in the church and the role of the Holy Spirit have not received much attention in the theology of the past few centuries, but at present they are the object of considerable discussion. This promises an enrichment, not just for ecclesiology, but also for the theology of the Incarnation and of the Trinity.

If the development of Catholic theology does follow the lines we have sketched, then it seems quite clear that there will be an increasing confrontation of Catholic thought with the contemporary intellectual world. Already there are clear signs—the summoning of Vatican II is one of the clearest—that Catholic scholars are probing with increased historical understanding into the deeper problems raised by Orthodoxy and the Reformation, prob-

lems that touch on the very nature of revealed religion, problems
that neither Orthodoxy nor the Reformation, nor the Catholic
reaction to these two, has completely solved. There should be,
moreover, an intensified grappling with the problem raised by the
influential flourishing of a-theistic thought in the past few centuries. What precisely will emerge from this increased contact
with non-Catholic thought no one can say; but Catholic theology
lives and grows by such contact, so it is not foolhardy to predict
for Catholic theology a period of development that promises to
be the most important in its history.

II

If the years ahead give promise of important developments in
Catholic thought, they give at least equal promise of growth in
the area of Catholic spirituality and worship. Biblical studies will
unquestionably have an ever larger influence in this regard, and
with this will come an increasing Christ-centeredness in the spirituality of the Catholic community. For example, there is every
reason to expect that, as present biblical theologizing about the
mystery of the resurrection filters down into popular understanding, it will intensify in the individual Christian and in the
church the awareness of Christ's presence. This greater awareness
in turn should lead to a greater sense of immediacy in prayer
directed to Christ, but also to a greater appreciation of the mystery of Christ's being as God-man. Scientific biblical studies, which
to the uneducated seem to threaten the reality and devotional impact of the New Testament events, will instead lead to sharper
accuracy and therefore to deeper reverence in the Catholic approach to the figure of the risen Lord.

As one looks ahead, it appears that this insistence on the focal
role of Jesus in the present mystery of the church and the Christian's life will necessarily place at the center of the Catholic's
religious consciousness a personal act of self-commitment to the
risen Christ. Hence in turn greater emphasis will be placed on the

role of freedom in the development of Christian spirituality; spiritual growth will be seen increasingly from the point of view of the maturing of Christian free choice, from the point of view of adult response to the divine initiative in grace. All this is not something entirely new: Catholic thought and life have always known that Christ must be freely accepted by the Christian in faith and love; yet too often this knowledge has tended to be translated in terms of conformity to laws and practices rather than of profound personal self-giving to a person. Such self-giving, if it does come to dominate a Christian's viewpoint, will also lead to deeper involvement in the betterment of human life.

Another element in the growth of Catholic spirituality is the new orientation in moral theology. The very fact that this topic can be classed as an integral part of our discussion of Christian spirituality indicates the extent of the reappraisal in which moral theologians are involved at the moment. Although there will always be a need to differentiate the various prudential applications of law to human behavior and a need to define for Christians the precise demands of their individual and social existence, present-day Catholic moral theology is moving away from too exclusive attention to casuistry. Triggered by books like Gilleman's *Primacy of Charity*, Catholic thought has in recent years laid much greater stress upon the role of love and free self-commitment in the development of the individual's moral structure. Moreover, in place of preoccupation with sexual morality, there is increased awareness of the need to develop a theology of the moral obligations which touch upon man's life in community, be it the family, the nation or an international community.

And instead of discussing Christian morality almost entirely in terms of sins to be avoided, moralists are insisting on the positive ideal that should govern Christian behavior. For this reason, moral theology and the clarification of Christian spirituality are more and more tending to become one area of knowledge in Catholic theological circles.

III

One of the most powerful influences affecting the present state of Catholic life and worship, one which is certain to continue into the immediate future, is the much heralded liturgical revival. There seems no question but that there is taking place a most important swing from a devotional emphasis on religion to the more basic Christian attitude of living out the sacraments. More advanced in some European countries but rapidly gaining ground in the United States, this liturgical revitalization has already had notable influence on architecture, sacred art and music, and is slowly having its impact on popular piety. As it gains ground— and it is doing so with increased official support—this movement will inevitably deepen and solidify the Christ-centeredness and personalist aspect already described; for the heart attitude of Eucharistic participation is a deep personal commitment to and union with Christ in his redemptive mysteries of death and resurrection.

Perhaps the most sensitive point in this movement away from excessive attention to devotional practices is the matter of Catholic devotion to Mary. Here one must be very careful to keep a balanced view, toward the intrinsic elements of Mariology and devotion to Mary and toward the new and recent tendencies in Catholic theology and devotional life. There can be no question but that some popular devotion to Mary has tended to become over-balanced and even to obscure the Christian devotedness to the more central mystery of Christ himself. However, one must also be careful not to judge the theological positions officially held by the Catholic Church and expounded by theologians with some of these popular trends toward exaggeration.

What is most encouraging about the present situation is the growing tendency to situate Mary herself in what is her correct position, within the church as its most eminent member, and to direct the attitude of Catholics toward Mary in terms of her role in the Christian community. All this will in no way deny the role of motherhood which is proper to Mary because of her unique relationship to Christ himself; it will tend to put the relationship of Mary as mother of Christians into its correct perspective. There are not only hopes, but good indications, that the Catholic people's devotion to Mary is becoming increasingly mature and consciously bound up with devotion to Christ himself. Unquestionably, the advance of the liturgical movement has been a great force in bringing about this change, and as it becomes more fully established, it will act, not to suppress devotion to Mary, but to situate it very solidly in the midst of the church's sacramental life and Christian worship of the Father.

Another factor of major importance as one appraises the present state of Catholic spirituality with an eye to its development in the next two decades is the growingly important role of the layman in the church's life. As the lay person becomes better educated in theological matters and more involved in living the mystery of the church's life, these will inevitably result in emphasis on elements in Christian living that have remained relatively undeveloped. Such a spirituality lived by the laity cannot be essentially monastic in tone; rather it must prepare the lay Christian for involvement in a world that is destined to be Christianized. As such, it will probably build a great deal on the present Catholic theological insistence that charity is the soul of true Christian living; it will flow, too, from a rapidly developing understanding of the sanctifying nature of Christian marriage. The layman's life and sanctity and apostolate in the church will unquestionably be the object of increased study and respect within the Catholic community in the years ahead.

IV

With this new role of the layman and the promise it gives of a new functioning of Christians in the life of the Catholic Church, one might ask about the extent of change that is likely to occur in the structural aspects of the Catholic community. Here it is very hard to assess what is taking place at the present time and what is likely to eventuate in the immediate future. While no major changes are anticipated in the Catholic Church's structure, the problems and progress of man in the late 20th century will have considerable impact upon many elements of parish life and diocesan structure and, perhaps more importantly, on the international organization of the Catholic Church. Though this will come quite gradually, there are already indications from the first two sessions of the Vatican Council that the eventual modifications may be quite sweeping.

The Catholic Church in the United States has always found its strength in the large urban centers of population. It will, then, inevitably be deeply affected by the increased urbanization of the human race. As people crowd more and more into these great urban communities, the Catholic Church will face the need to appraise the validity of the traditional parish organization. In such depersonalized mass existence, in the densely populated inner city which in many ways resembles an untapped mission field, the usual parish structure may be replaced by some other more flexible approach. There are serious indications that those responsible for the evangelization of the inner city are beginning to think of new methods which would be better adapted to the precise needs of the people who dwell there.

Obviously, a very critical aspect of this problem deals with the Catholic school system. To an extent which is absolutely unique in the history of the Catholic Church the Roman Catholic community of the United States has centered its structural development around the Catholic school. In many parishes it is the school which tends to be the center of focus. As the financial burden of the Catholic school system mounts—and there is no present indication that the burden will be decreased—and as the precise objectives and needs for Catholic schooling are modified because of the changing sociological situation of American Catholics, one wonders what precisely will be the pattern of the Catholic school a decade or two decades from now. And if the role of the Catholic school does begin to change, this will inevitably dictate a reconsideration of the life of the American Catholic parish. It is unlikely that one will see the Catholic school system vanish from the American scene, but it is not too unlikely that it will become a more selective approach to education, and that the role of lay people both as teachers and as administrators will become increasingly prominent and important. This, in turn, will very likely lead to a closer relationship between the Catholic school system and the public schools of the country.

V

This increasing prominence of the lay Catholic gives clear promise of a greater involvement of the Catholic community in American social, political and cultural life. Some, of course, may fear that such involvement would mean a factional activity of the Roman Catholic Church operating as a bloc with purely confessional interests. What is much more likely to come to pass is an increasing maturity on the part of educated Catholic laity and clergy regarding their responsibilities for a wider political, educational and social context of American and international life. Catholic social thought represents a rich heritage upon which the thought and life of the United States could draw with great benefit. But such a contribution of Catholics to the American situation can come about only if there be greater involvement of educated Catholic laity in all the spheres—professional, educational, political, social, religious—of American life. The growing number of well educated and influential Catholics gives promise that this will happen.

One can also expect an increasing involvement of Catholics in the intellectual life of the American people—not only because of the rising social situation of the Catholic population and the resulting increase of higher education among Catholics, but also because of more "conversation" between Catholic colleges and universities and other institutions of higher learning in the country.

Thus far intellectual interchange between Catholic schools and others is only in its beginning stage, but prospects for its growth are quite encouraging.

Much the same kind of growth will probably mark the attitude of Catholics toward the international scene. More and more aware of the deeper dimensions of Christianization, Catholic missionary effort is being directed with increasing emphasis toward the analysis, criticism and Christian transformation of societal patterns and institutions. Obviously, this will mean that Catholics who devote themselves to bringing the message and the charity of Christ to the culturally turbulent areas of Asia, Africa and South America must be prepared to immerse themselves in the total life pattern of those peoples. Awareness of the profound preparation required in one who would undertake such a task should be an important incentive to the Catholic, layman or cleric, to develop true maturity of faith, and along with it a genuine professional proficiency in those fields of human learning—economics, sociology, medicine, etc. which will enable him to help peoples of other lands to build a more truly human existence for themselves.

Perhaps one could summarize the deepening social involvement of the American Catholic community by saying that it is more positively coming to grips with the world around it—with the world of scientific and technological advance, with the world of informational (if not educational) progress, with the world of great cultural and social and religious pluralism. There can always be the danger for Catholics, because of their essential commitment to the greater value of the life beyond, that they will undercommit themselves to the betterment of the present life. More and more it seems that American Catholics are escaping this danger, are realizing that Christianity is truly eschatological in the sense that the world to come will develop out of the Christianization of the world which is, and are increasingly accepting the role of living the truth and the charity of Christ in the midst of their brethren.

13. THE ORTHODOX: ARRIVAL AND DIALOGUE

John S. Romanides*

The appearance of Orthodox churches in the western hemisphere, particularly in the United States and Canada, could prove to be one of the most important factors in the current move toward Christian unity. That may seem a strange credit to impute to the relatively late insertion of 5 million or so Orthodox Christians into a religious and cultural complex made up of some 100 million Protestants and Roman Catholics. But to the Orthodox theologian it is obvious, and it will become more clear as Orthodoxy completes her evolution from the status of immigrant to that of native American church, a process that will render her capable of interpreting herself to her new neighbors.

The United States and Canada are the only non-Orthodox countries with Orthodox populations large enough for sustained dialogue to be carried on with earlier established Protestant and Roman Catholic groups. Such opportunity is unique in Christian history; it should be taken seriously and utilized. A short article is not the place to spell out in detail the possibilities of such dialogue. But it may be helpful, for the sake of striking up acquaintance between Protestants and Roman Catholics and their Orthodox neighbors, to say a few things about Orthodoxy in the western hemisphere, her problems, and the possibilities relating to her arrival as an American church and her role in a divided Christendom.

In the last quarter of the 18th century an Orthodox mission was established by Russians in Alaska. Today, in spite of the

* Professor Romanides is a member of the faculty of Holy Cross Greek Orthodox Theological School, Brookline, Massachusetts.

problems created by the Russian revolution and by the activities of non-Orthodox missions, Orthodoxy is still the religion of a large portion of Alaska's native population.

I

Within the United States and Canada there was no more than a handful of Orthodox until the last quarter of the 19th century, when substantial groups of Greek Orthodox and Uniate Greek Catholics began immigrating from central and southeastern Europe, the Near East and Africa. The Uniates from central Europe were descended from Orthodox Christians who had been brought under control of the papacy in the late 16th century through political and social pressures exerted by the ruling Roman Catholics in Poland and the Austro-Hungarian empire.

As the 19th century opened the Uniates were more numerous in the United States than the Orthodox. However, many of them, recalling their Orthodox background and the way their ancestors had come under papal control, started what turned out to be a major revolution against the papacy. They asked to be admitted to the jurisdiction of the Russian Orthodox archdiocese and were accepted. Meanwhile, the archdiocese had been moved to San Francisco (in 1872); with increased Orthodox immigration to the east coast it was moved to New York to facilitate administration of the new churches. Today this church counts on its rolls nearly 1 million members.

Though movement of the Uniates back to Orthodoxy was blunted somewhat by the turmoil created among Slavic Christians by the communist revolution in Russia, it did not stop. The Greeks, who had arrived in great number between 1900 and 1926, received into their jurisdiction (Constantinople) about 100 Ukranian and Carpathorussian Uniate parishes which have since attained a combined membership of some 200,000, organized into two groups. From time to time other Uniate groups find their way back to the Orthodox fold; of the around 5 million Orthodox now in the

United States, between 800,000 and 1 million are either former Uniates or descendants of Uniates.

What turned out to be the largest single Orthodox church in the United States owes her growth to Greek immigration—from the kingdom of Greece, the Ottoman empire (parts of which were added to Greece and other Balkan countries or became part of the Turkish republic), Cyprus, the Dodecanese islands (Italian possession), Egypt, Palestine, Albania, Serbia, Bulgaria, Romania and Russia. Of the approximately 1.5 million Greek Orthodox in the United States, perhaps half are here as the result of political and social disruptions created by the Balkan wars and expulsion from the newly formed Turkish republic of some 2 million Greeks.

The third largest Orthodox immigration stemmed from Russia proper and from the Ukraine, followed in size by immigrations from Yugoslavia, Syria, Lebanon, Bulgaria, Romania, Albania and Poland. A few thousand have come, too, from such lands as Estonia, Latvia, Lithuania, Czechoslovakia and Finland.

The largest group of non-Chalcedonian Orthodox in the United States is made up of Armenians, followed by the Syrian Jacobites, the Ethopians and the Copts (from Egypt). Differing from the Chalcedonian Orthodox only in christological terminology, they have a worldwide membership of between 30 and 40 million, bringing the total world membership of non-Protestant, non-Roman Catholic Christians to some 250 million. Both Chalcedonian and non-Chalcedonian Orthodox are united in witness to the faith of the ancient church and for all practical purposes have presented a united theological voice in dialogue with Protestants in the World Council of Churches.

II

Although perhaps 75 per cent of the world's Orthodox rarely encounter Protestants or Roman Catholics, *all* of them know about those two groups from their catechism, their national literature and their history courses, which as a matter of course cover such topics as the Roman schism, the crusades and the Reformation. In contrast, the average American is only of late becoming aware of the existence of Orthodox Christianity. Recently I spent the time it took to get a haircut trying to explain to the barber how one could be a Christian without being Roman Catholic or Protestant.

The situation is not so surprising when one notes in a book titled *Chats with Prospective Converts* (written by Father M. D. Forest, with a preface by Bishop Fulton J. Sheen) the surprising statement that the Orthodox church "comprises only some oriental races, especially Greeks" (page 44). At fault too are deficiencies in the teaching of Roman, medieval and European history in the public schools, teaching which leaves pupils unaware that Orthodoxy was the religion of the citizens of the Roman empire until its collapse in 1453, just 30 years before the birth of Martin Luther, and that it remains the religion of more than 100 million Europeans, to say nothing of "orientals."

Such ignorance on the part of the general public has had some serious consequences in the lives of Orthodox Americans. Only since World War II have Orthodox members of the armed forces been privileged to have their religious designation placed on their identification tags, which previously recognized only Roman Catholics, Protestants and Jews, with other veterans marked off as having "other" or "no" religion. More than anything else, it was the "dog tag" experience of World War II that led Orthodox veterans and their families to press their leaders into organized efforts to have Orthodoxy recognized as the nation's fourth major faith. Not only has the identification tag situation been resolved, but Orthodox chaplains have been added to the armed forces roster.

A supporting factor in Orthodox determination to be recognized as a major faith is the cultural, social and political disability associated with non-recognition. For instance, the Greeks are puzzled by the fact that while so many Americans—to say nothing of their history textbooks and their periodicals—are at great pains to recognize Western civilization's indebtedness to Greece, they pay little attention to the Christian form of Greek civilization.

Some Greeks jokingly suggest that had they remained faithful to the gods of Mount Olympus, Greek paganism might have long since been recognized as the fourth major faith in the United States.

Still another prod to the Orthodox drive for recognition has been the example set by the Jews, who do not greatly exceed the Orthodox in number of nominal and practicing adherents; indeed, the number of *practicing* Orthodox may be as great if not greater. The Jews have of course not had to overcome general ignorance of the mere fact of their existence, but they have been much more aggressive in asserting their right to equal status. Perhaps partly because the Jews are not fellow Christians, many if not most Protestant and Catholic leaders have been very active in helping them achieve such status—yet I know of no major Protestant or Roman Catholic religious leader or writer who has taken up the cause of Orthodox recognition.

Achievement of full status as a major American faith might mean more fair play, particularly in regard to proselyting tactics which take advantage of the socially weak position of many Orthodox. I must say that on the whole Protestants have abandoned such tactics in favor of creating an atmosphere of dialogue. But in recent years Roman Catholics have spent millions of dollars beefing up the Uniate movement in America and intensifying anti-Orthodox activity—a crusade which they consider an expression of love but which in Orthodox eyes is a sure sign that after 400 years Roman Catholics still mistake their own thoughts and feelings for those of others.

In spite of this and similar crusades, with the return to Orthodoxy of close to 1 million Uniates in America and 9 million in central Europe there are probably not more than 1 million Uniates of Chalcedonian background left in the Roman Catholic Church. One would think that by now Rome would have changed her attitude to the Orthodox to one of dialogue, particularly since the illiterate peasant who could be confused by identity of ritual is almost a thing of the past. The claim that the Uniate defections

from Rome in central Europe were due to communist pressure
may well be true, and if so the fact is to be regretted. But the
uncoerced and in most cases unsolicited return in America of
Uniates who originated from the same part of Europe opens up
the possibility that coercion in that area was not as great as has
been claimed.

This year all Orthodox youth organizations in America ar-
ranged their conventions and summer activities to coincide in
Pittsburgh, culminating in a Pan-Orthodox festival on August 31.
The purpose of that festival, which was attended by 11,000 youth
leaders and other representatives, was to emphasize Orthodox solidarity in the United States, to draw attention to the determination
to achieve recognition as a major faith, and (indirectly) to inform
Roman Catholics, with their Uniate propaganda center in Pittsburgh, that the Orthodox are in America to stay.

III

For several decades Protestants and Roman Catholics (particularly the latter) have emphasized the jurisdictional alignments
along ethnic lines of Orthodoxy in America and elsewhere in order
to point a finger at what they consider disunity and "nationalism."
Limited by their own understanding of unity as involving merger
(Protestant) or centralization (Roman Catholic), they fail to
discern how the Orthodox themselves view Christian unity, and
to appreciate how oneness of the Orthodox in faith and worship
constitutes a union which transcends such cultural diversities as
exist, sometimes even within a single or ethnic group.

Since immigration laws are highly prejudicial toward those
countries from which Orthodox Christians are likely to come
(Greece's annual quota, for instance, is only 317), the number of
foreign-born Orthodox in this country will be reduced to in-
significance within the next decade or two. American-born Orthodox already constitute about 80 per cent of the total membership.
That this trend will accelerate the disappearance of the jurisdic-

tional alignments based on ethnic distinctions is realized even by those who would prefer not to see such a development.

Several years ago the fifty or so immigrant bishops in the United States formed a Standing Conference of Orthodox Bishops; the youth organizations followed, forming the Conference of Eastern Orthodox Youth Leaders of America. For many years local inter-jurisdictional and interethnic clerical associations have been in existence. Since in general the Orthodox have deep respect and admiration for each other's cultural traditions, such associations are concerned not so much with cultural homogeneity as with ecclesiastical cooperation within the framework of cultural diversity.

IV

For some time Orthodox leaders have been expounding or suggesting various ideas in regard to the future jurisdictional and linguistic form of the American Orthodox churches. At present the situation is complicated by the fact that many of the countries of origin are under communist rule. Some 1.5 million of such Orthodox have assumed de facto independence. Another 1.7 million Greeks, Ukranians, Carpathorussians and Albanians are under the jurisdiction of the Ecumenical Patriarchate of Constantinople. The Syrian, Bulgarian, Serbian and Romanian churches are under the jurisdiction of the patriarchates in the countries of their origin.

Recently the Patriarchate of Moscow sought to restore relations with the Russian Orthodox Greek Catholic Church in America. As an inducement it offered a form of de facto autonomy such as that church has already assumed, thus ensuring it against political involvement with the Soviet government. Nevertheless, the offer was turned down. Orthodox Americans who are under the jurisdiction of patriarchates under the Islamic rule are not interested in any jurisdictional scheme which would tend to weaken Orthodoxy in those areas. It is to be hoped that the Patriarchate of

Moscow will avoid involving the American Orthodox in what is (perhaps erroneously) reported to be an attempt on its part to assert leadership in the Orthodox world.

Nevertheless, determination of continuing Orthodox coordination in America will remain with the already established Standing Conference of Orthodox Bishops, which in time may evolve into a Synod of the Orthodox Catholic Church in the U.S.A., under the spiritual leadership of the Ecumenical Patriarchate of Constantinople but with each group continuing the ties which it now enjoys or wishes to enjoy with its mother church.

Many Orthodox leaders in America believe that English should be used as the primary medium of worship, in keeping with Orthodoxy's tradition which calls for the use of native languages. Others would like to see preservation in worship of the language of the New Testament, or the ancient language of their respective churches, or simply the language brought to America by their fathers or grandfathers. English has become the primary language for preaching, Sunday School teaching and administration in all Orthodox churches, and the secondary language for worship in all but one. It has become the primary, and in many cases the only, liturgical language in the Syrian Orthodox churches, and the only one in those churches comprised entirely of converts—some of which have preserved their Western liturgical traditions and whose members are sometimes referred to as Western Rite Orthodox.

V

The administrative form which Orthodox Christianity will assume in America will be determined by her commitment to her own history, which she traces in unbroken succession to the primitive Church. Since this history guides her in her relations with both Roman Catholics and Protestants, it would be helpful to discuss certain aspects of Orthodox unity and administration which have a direct bearing on Orthodox attitudes toward the future in America and toward prospects of Christian unity.

Perhaps a fruitful approach would be to begin with the Orthodox definition of the Church which was adopted by the Fourth World Conference On Faith And Order in Montreal. According to this definition one should not think of local congregations as part of the One Church. Rather the Universal Church is "the Body of Christ, including the saints of all ages and Christians of all places, which is both present in and one with the local congregation gathered for the hearing of the Word and the celebration of the Eucharist. . . ." Thus, St. Ignatius of Antioch (d. 117 A.D.) declared that "Wherever Jesus Christ is there is the Catholic Church." This means that "each church or congregation participating in Christ is related to others not by participation in some higher structure or organization but rather by an identity of existence in Christ. In this sense each congregation gathered for the proclamation of the Word and the celebration of the Eucharist is a manifestation of the whole Catholic Church in the very process of becoming what she is in service and witness to the world."

This identity of existence in Christ of all congregations eating of the One Bread and drinking of the One Cup means that there can be no sacramental subordination of one congregation to another. The fullness of Christ and his Body, the Universal Church of all ages and all places, is one with each local congregation, which in turn is one with the Universal Church. That the total Christ is present in each congregation in this way is vividly pointed to by the Greek Patristic tradition which applies the Pauline image of the Church as the Body of Christ and Christ as the Head of the Body to the local congregation. The local gathering of the faithful is a manifestation of the total Christ, Body and Head. The head of the Eucharistic Assembly is the image of Christ as the Head, and his spiritual children are the image of Christ as the Body. According to the Old Testament and St. Paul, Christ, the Lord of Glory, the Head, is the Bridegroom and his Body, Israel, is his Bride. Thus Orthodox ordinations are likened to marriage between clergy and the congregation, as between Christ and the Church, and the transfer of clergy is strictly forbidden by the canons and likened to acts of adultery.

It is in the light of this understanding of the Church that

Orthodox architecture and icons of Christ, the Virgin, and the saints must be understood. The icons and the architecture of the Church make visually manifest, and constantly remind the faithful of, the presence of Christ and his Body, the Universal Church of all ages and all places. This total Christ is included in the call to love one another. Orthodox Christians are scandalized by Protestant indifference to love for the mother of Christ and the saints, and many feel that this lack alone makes doubtful their salvation, since without love of neighbor (which includes the saints of all ages), there can be no salvation.

In the ancient Church each Eucharistic Assembly was headed by a bishop. Very early these bishops organized themselves into synods whose jurisdiction was determined by the provincial divisions of the Roman Empire. The provincial synods gathered together at the ordinations of the bishops and at regular intervals at the provincial capitals. Since the bishop of the provincial capital was usually the host at the gatherings of the bishops, he was recognized as the presiding bishop of the provincial synod and became known as the Metropolitan. The bishops decided upon questions by vote in synod and not by the arbitrary rule of any one bishop. The Metropolitan was *primus inter pares*.

When the Roman provinces were later reorganized and grouped into dioceses, the bishops of the diocesan capitals were recognized as having a primacy of honor (*primus inter pares*) above that of the provincial Metropolitans. Then there was a higher scale of primacy of honor for those bishops of imperial capitals. Rome was given the first place (*primus inter pares*), Alexandria, the capital of the Ptolemies, was accorded second place, and Antioch, the capital of the Seleucid Empire, third place.

This regrouping of the provinces into dioceses gave rise to the distinction between autonomous and autocephalous groupings of bishops. Generally, the Roman dioceses became the basis of modifying, in most cases, the older autocephalous provincial synods which remained autonomous. For all practical purposes autocephalicity and autonomy meant the same thing, since in both instances self-government was carefully preserved. All bishops within each diocesan and provincial synodical grouping were elected and ordained without any interference from other provincial or diocesan synods. However, there came into existence a difference between the manner of ordaining the presiding bishop of an autocephalous synod and the presiding bishop of an autonomous synod. The head of an autocephalous synod was elected by the clergy and people of his own city and then ordained by the bishops of his own provincial or diocesan grouping. The head of an autonomous synod was also elected by the clergy and people of his own city, but his ordination was presided over by the head bishop of the autocephalous synod under whose surveillance his autonomous synod was assigned. This is clearly indicated by the 28th canon of the Fourth Ecumenical Council (451) which determined the three Roman dioceses (Thrace, Asiana, and Pontus) whose Metropolitans were to continue to be elected in the traditional way, but ordained by the bishop of New Rome (Constantinople). In contrast to this arrangement, Palestine and Cyprus remained autocephalous even though they were within the diocese of the East, presided over by the bishop of Antioch.

It is very important to bear in mind that most of the autocephalous and autonomous synods of ancient Christianity existed within one united Roman Empire. In other words, Christendom within the Roman Empire never understood Christian unity in terms of administrative, centralized organizational union common to Roman Catholicism and Protestant Denominationalism.

The adaptation of the ancient Church's synodical administration to Roman political institutions has always remained a principle in the history of Orthodox Christianity. The first serious challenge to this principle came with the development of the papacy in two stages.

The first stage of papal development was in reaction against the third canon of the Second Ecumenical Council (381), which declared that because New Rome (Constantinople) is the new capital of the Empire her bishop has an equal primacy of honor with the bishop of Old Rome. Since by this time Milan had taken the place of Old Rome as the seat of imperial administration over the Western provinces, the bishop of Rome was threatened by such reasoning with the loss of his primacy in Italy. His defense at a council of Rome in 382 was the claim that the primacies of Old Rome, Alexandria, and Antioch were based on their being founded by St. Peter (Rome and Antioch) or St. Mark (Alexandria), a disciple of St. Peter, and not on their being capital cities. No explanation was given as to why Antioch, founded by St. Peter himself, should be after and not before Alexandria, founded by St. Peter's disciple, and why other Churches founded by St. Peter and St. Mark should not also share in these primacies.

Very significant for the understanding of Orthodox administrative principles is the fact that the bishop of Jerusalem was for three centuries only a member of the provincial synod of Palestine presided over by the Metropolitan of the capital city of Caesarea. Since Palestine had been incorporated as one of the provinces of the Roman diocese of the East, the ordination (but not the election) of the Metropolitan of Caesarea (and of the Archbishop of Cyprus) should have been presided over by the Patriarch of Antioch. However, Jerusalem was finally made the capital city of the province of Palestine, which ecclesiastically was recognized as autocephalous. The Fourth Ecumenical Council (451) recognized the bishop of Palestine as the fifth Patriarch of the Empire having the fifth place of honor after the Patriarchs of Old Rome, New Rome (Constantinople), Alexandria, and Antioch. The Third Ecumenical Council (431) recognized the Churches of the Island of Cyprus as having been autocephalous since apostolic times and thus turned down Antioch's claim to preside over the ordination of the Archbishop of Cyprus based on the fact that the island was politically governed from the diocesan capital of Antioch.

The second stage of Old Rome's challenge to the administrative principles built into the canon law of the ancient Ecumenical Councils unfolded with the tremendous impact which feudal political theories had on the evolution of the papacy. The appointment of bishops to be vassal lords over the domains of the Holy Roman Empire of the Germans by the Frankish and German Emperors led to the control and corruption of the Church by the State. The reform movements which resulted based their hopes of cleaning house on the transference of episcopal appointments and vassalages from the kings of Europe to the Pope. Thus, a relationship of vassal Lords to the suzerain developed between the bishops of the West and the Pope. One can perhaps admire the struggle for the freedom of the Church underlying the strict clericalism and centralization which developed out of the struggles between Church and State in the West. But to pass all this off as the work of the Holy Spirit for the *whole Church* is for the Orthodox, whose many autocephalous and autonomous synods existed since very ancient times and who were never affected by the problems of a feudal society, incomprehensible. When the papacy attempted to impose ecclesiastical feudalism on the many autocephalous and autonomous Churches of the East, so often by the use of force during the crusades and later by the pressure of Polish and Austro-Hungarian power, a dogmatic and psychological rupture took place which will not be healed until the papacy recognizes the ecclesiological principles of the undivided Church of the ancient Ecumenical Councils.

What is especially disturbing to the Orthodox theologians engaged in ecumenical conversations concerning Christian unity is the fact that so many Protestants think of union in Roman Catholic terms of centralization by way of mergers and the setting up of world denominational alliances. The Orthodox are especially perturbed when they see their own administrative principles of autocephalicity and autonomy described in terms of disunity.

VI

The transposition of the Roman Orthodox principles of ecclesiology and synodical administration to the American scene would mean the existence of a bishop in each Eucharistic Assembly, or at least in each city, town and village. The provincial synods within the Roman Empire would be equivalent to county synods presided over by the bishops of the county seats who would be called Metropolitans. These would be autonomous Churches as described above. The Roman dioceses would be somewhat equivalent to our States. The presiding bishop of that county which contained the capital city of the state would preside over his own provincial synod which would be autocephalous and at the same time he would preside over the ordination, but not the election, of the county Metropolitans within the State. The bishops of State capitals would probably be called Archbishops.

The bishop of Washington would be recognized as the presiding bishop of his own county or District of Columbia synod. He would be called a Patriarch and would have a primacy of honor, but no jurisdiction, among all the bishops of the United States. Perhaps he would be accorded the privilege of presiding at the ordinations of the Archbishops and Metropolitans of Virginia and Maryland, but he would have no say in their election. If Canada and Mexico were to be included in an American Empire, then the bishops of their capital cities would be recognized as Patriarchs having the second and third places of honor after the Patriarch of Washington. If Orthodoxy in its ancient form were the religion of the Thirteen States at the time of the Revolutionary War, New York City would have been equivalent to Old Rome and Washington to New Rome (Constantinople). After the capital was moved the Patriarch of New York City might have feared the loss of his position of honor, especially since the capital of New York State was Albany, and searched around for a basis of his primacy other than that of having been at one time the bishop of the capital of the United States.

The above outline of synodical Church administration would be ideal for the ultimate future of Orthodoxy in America, and would be even more suited for any eventual union of all Christians in the United States. As in the Orthodox Churches throughout the world, there would be unity in faith and worship, but not in terms of administrative centralization which never existed in Biblical and Ancient Christendom.

In the course of history the Orthodox Churches modified their canonical or Roman structure of Church administration, while remaining faithful to the general principles of the autonomy and autocephalicity of the ancient provincial and diocesan synods. The earliest variations of her synodical structures were the existence of the national Churches of Armenia, Egypt, and Ethiopia, where autocephalicity and autonomy were based on national identity. In the Middle Ages there arose the autocephalous national Churches of Georgia, Bulgaria and Serbia and in the beginning of the modern age the autocephalous Church of Russia and finally the rest of the many autocephalous and autonomous Churches of the last two centuries. These autocephalous and autonomous synods differ from those of the Roman Empire in that they are each coterminous with a whole nation and are not one of several autocephalous Churches within one nation or ethnic group.

The only exceptions to this identity of autocephalicity and autonomy with ethnic identity are to be found today among the Greeks. They comprise, in some cases with Arabs, the six autocephalous Churches of Constantinople, Alexandria, Jerusalem, Cyprus, Sinai, and Greece, and the two autonomous Churches of the Islands of Crete and the Dodecanese. Within the Soviet Union there are three autocephalous Churches of the Russians, Georgians and Armenians.

Thus, there are two possible administrative patterns which the Orthodox Churches in the United States may follow: (1) the one with several autocephalous and autonomous synods within one nation, or (2) the one with one national synod within one nation. This means that there is nothing basically wrong with the present existence of several Orthodox jurisdictions in America. However, the situation is unique and uncanonical, not because of multiplicity of jurisdictions, as has been pointed out, but because of geographical overlapping based on national origin. All realize that this is of a temporary nature and changes are expected in the near future. The Standing Conference of American Orthodox Bishops is an advanced move in this direction.

The one important factor which makes very unlikely the possibility of there eventually being several autocephalous regional or State synods in the United States is the fact that for many years the non-Greek Churches of the Orthodox World have become accustomed to the idea of each ethnic group being one single autocephalous or autonomous Church. Also for many centuries the Orthodox have become accustomed to cities, towns and villages without bishops. Thus, the provincial synod presided over by the provincial Metropolitan or Archbishop has almost completely disappeared, except on the Islands of Cyprus, Crete and the Dodecanese.

VII

From an Orthodox point of view many aspects of Roman Catholic-Protestant differences are really divergent consequences of similar, sometimes identical, presuppositions. This means that on several key issues the Orthodox consider dialogue between Roman Catholics and Protestants really soliloquy which can become true dialogue only when the Orthodox are included.

Such three-way dialogue might help break down the thousand-year-old impasse between the Latin and Greek churches. Thus far two-way dialogue between those two groups has proved impossible because each has interpreted the other's theological language according to his own categories. For instance, the Greeks rejected the dogmatic formula of Filioque (that the Holy Spirit proceeds from the Son as well as from the Father) because, according to their categories—which are those of the First (325) and the Second (381) Ecumenical Councils—it is sheer heresy. On the other hand, the Latins in a legalistic way accepted the decisions of those Greek councils as authority, but with little understanding of the cate-

gories dominating the lengthy debates which provided background. One calls to mind St. Augustine's complaint that he could
not understand what the Greeks meant by distinguishing between
essence and hypostasis in the Trinity (*De Trinitate*, v, 8, 10), and
this happens to be one of the foundation stones of Greek Trinitarian theology. When difficulties arose about the Filioque the
Latins, consistent with their trinitarian categories, insisted that it
is a dogma of faith necessary for salvation. The seventh century
Greek theologian St. Maximus the Confessor calmed Greek sus-
picions by translating the Filioque into Greek categories. The
enthusiasm of later Frankish and Latin theologians led the West
to claim that the Filioque is consistent with and implicit in the
decisions of the early Greek Ecumenical Councils, even that it was
taught by the Greek Fathers. For a while the Latins accused the
Greeks of having removed the Filioque from the Creed and thus
having betrayed their own tradition. Eventually they repeated that
accusation in regard to other aspects of doctrine on which differences exist—such as grace, merits, sacraments, purgatory, authority, ecclesiology, even piety. The practical effect of many
centuries of such anti-Greek propaganda has been to create a Latin
image of the Greek as a stubborn and tricky churchman who because of pride refuses to be faithful to his own tradition.

There is, however, another Latin approach to the Orthodox
which for many years has existed parallel to the one described
above, with one or the other emphasized as situations vary. According to this view, the Orthodox *have* remained faithful to their
own Greek tradition and in essentials do not differ from Roman
Catholics. Judging from reports of recent statements by Pope
Paul VI, this approach will be emphasized during his pontificate.

All in all, however, until Roman Catholics are prepared (and
there are signs that some may be) to entertain seriously the possibility that the Orthodox have remained faithful to their own
tradition and that this tradition is not identical with that of the
medieval West, there can be no real dialogue. Orthodox theologians are prepared to accept the legitimacy of the expression

of the Christian faith in categories other than those of the Ecumenical Councils—provided that those categories confess the same
faith and point the way to the same soteriological experience.
Further, if Rome truly desires dialogue, she must once and for
all realize that the propaganda approach to the Uniates is not a
bridge between East and West but a wall of separation.

In sharp contrast to the Roman Catholic-Orthodox stalemate
(interrupted only by a trickle of private discussion in isolated
groups) Protestant-Orthodox dialogue seems to have entered a new
phase at the Fourth World Conference on Faith and Order held in
Montreal last summer. At their first separate "nocturnal meeting"
the Orthodox decided unanimously to do everything possible to
avoid issuing a separate statement. As it turned out, not only were
they pleased with results of their discussions with Protestants in
section and subsection discussions, but they discovered that they
could offer explanations and even write theological definitions
which Protestants accepted as valid expression of their own con-
victions. The same thing happened with certain Protestant explanations and statements which the Orthodox could accept. The
possibility of a converging of minds was demonstrated in discussions on the nature of the church, tradition and worship.

On the whole, however, the Orthodox found in the fact that
categories of discussion were predominantly Protestant a continuous source of irritation. The only really sour note was struck by
one subcommittee's description of the "ecclesial character" of
the World Council of Churches as "somehow" sharing in the oneness, holiness, catholicity and apostolicity of the church or of
churches. This view the Orthodox opposed—and they were gratified to note that their "nocturnal meeting" on the question was
supported by a Protestant rooting section.

At an informal gathering in Montreal of the Greek delegates
the lack of episcopacy in certain Protestant churches was discussed;
it was agreed that if occasion arose the Greeks would suggest to
the other Orthodox delegates that support might be given to any

scheme of union which accepted the actual existence of a bishop in each local congregation, in keeping with the practice of the ancient church—so long as the threefold ministry was maintained, together with the right of each church to continue or to determine its tradition or practice on this question. It was felt that such an approach might facilitate union among churches of British background by helping overcome the problems raised by the historic Anglican position on the episcopacy.

It became evident in the discussions at Montreal that the Calvinist understanding of apostolic succession in terms of doctrinal purity, rather than the Roman Catholic and Anglican emphasis on the mechanics of continuous ordinations, is similar at least to the most important aspect of Orthodox understanding: that since apostolic succession belongs to the church and since only within the church can one share in it, upon leaving the church one does not take it with him.

Though agreements and understandings have been reached and an atmosphere of dialogue established between Orthodox and Protestants, real gaps remain; they stem from essential differences in presuppositions. To implement the findings of the Orthodox-Protestant consultation which immediately preceded the Montreal conference, a common study of biblical and ancient Christian presuppositions is to be undertaken in the hope that a more realistic picture of the history of divergences between the Latin and Greek traditions may be arrived at. One of the most beneficial results of the consultation and of the conference itself was the realization of how much caricature is passed off as Orthodox by some Protestants, and vice versa. A common desire was expressed for an exchange of theological professors so each group can become better acquainted with the other's tradition.

From my recent experience at a colloquium between Roman Catholics and Orthodox at St. Mary's University in San Antonio, Texas, I would suggest that Roman Catholic-Orthodox dialogue is possible within a similar framework. Perhaps the day is not far off when a three-way dialogue will have become reality, especially since the meeting between the bishops of Old Rome and New Rome in Jerusalem.

14. EPISCOPALIANS: MUDDLING THROUGH VS. CREATIVE OUTREACH

C. Kilmer Myers*

For many in the American church community the Episcopal Church is an enigma. It also is the source of frequent irritation. The reason often given for this situation is Anglicanism's apparent inability to decide whether it is essentially catholic or protestant. Indeed, in the view of some observers, far from fusing the two traditions into a creative synthesis, which is its claim, this church succeeds only in meaningless compromise. Given the fact that political rather than theological considerations effect most such compromises, one might well define Anglicanism as a religious community bent on not rocking the boat. There are many ways of not rocking the boat, and no doubt Anglicanism has discovered them all. Among us Episcopalians not rocking is called "muddling through."

From another perspective, however, the enigmatic character of the Episcopal Church (and the Anglican Communion) may stem from its being probably the freest church in the world. Almost anything goes—providing its appearance is decent and orderly. Had British Bishop John A. T. Robinson read his *Honest to God* while wearing a cope and miter and seated upon his cathedra, the conservative *Church Times* no doubt would have given the celebrated essay a fair review.

* Dr. Myers, an Episcopal priest, is director of the Urban Training Center for Christian Mission, an interdenominational project centering in Chicago.

1

There is a truth here not always grasped by nonconformity, a truth perhaps best put in a bit of counsel given his students by the late William Palmer Ladd of Berkeley Divinity School: "If you are a catholic you can be anything!" And so you can. Being a "catholic" within Anglicanism means that one recognizes within the historical continuum of the church's life a kind of mystical glue that keeps things together, and never better than when a lot of muddling is going on. Paul Tillich talks about the "catholic substance," but this is not really the same as the mysterious (albeit pragmatic) glue. You can never put your finger on that glue even though you know it's there. You are chary about becoming overly definitive about it; you simply assume it's always there somehow holding things together. A good Anglican *must* believe in it. He may then do as he pleases and say what he likes. It's rather a good church to belong to!

If the "glue" theory of the nature of their church is correct, Episcopalians in the days ahead will give a great deal of attention to that theory. Already it is producing a new type of churchmanship which presently defies precise definition. This churchmanship is neither catholic nor protestant although—depending on the mood and the circumstance—it sometimes appears to be both. It looks to the *mysterium* at the center of the church's being and tends to regard this as part of the "given" in the situation. One does not play lightly with the given; he accepts it or rejects it. He apprehends it in faith—or perhaps one should say that he is "grasped" by that which is given. Is the elusive glue the given *mysterium*? A mood akin to agnosticism ordinarily appears when this question is raised. The certainty is that whatever it is, it is there; we accept it and can then get on with the business.

Cognizant of this the new churchman seeks new meanings of the episcopate as part of the given. He understands that the bishop is before all else a sacramental person. To break through to this understanding is difficult in these days when the image of the bishop is that of an administrative functionary dressed up in Elizabethan court clothes. No longer is the bishop a prince (although we still have a few who imagine they are), nor is he chosen out of the ranks because of his undoubted sanctity. Today a priest is made a bishop because his acculturation quotient is high; i.e., he has been the successful rector of an effective parish. An examination of the roster of what the *Episcopal Church Annual* calls living American bishops indicates, of course, that this is not always true. It is, however, true enough to merit some thought.

Now all this is beginning to be questioned. What has happened to the episcopate? Who are bishops? What is their place in the *mysterium* and/or glue, and what is their role in the church's mission and ministry to mass society? These questions are raised against the background of developing ecumenism and the demands of mission in an urbanized society. If Anglicans continue to insist on episcopacy as a necessary ingredient for reunion, they had better put forth something better than administrators with fancy titles. They will need to look deeply into the historical and theological meanings of the office of bishop in the church of God. And they will need to ponder anew the bishop's role in metropolitan society. It may well be that the development of a truly "urban" theology will lead to new insights into the meaning of *episcopos*. Bishops and cities belong together. Great bishops like Bayne, Warnecke and Emrich, themselves able theologians and church strategists, will lead the way in this, and the new churchmen will follow gladly.

II

Episcopalians will become ecumenically involved. The growing intensity of this engagement will derive from two important factors. The first is the arrival of a substantial body of both clergy and laity on a plateau of catholicity which is unselfconscious and not easily threatened. These people "wear it well." It was not long ago that the so-called catholic revival in American Episcopalianism was forever on the defensive—which is quite understandable in view of the now freely admitted fact that so much that was being defended really was indefensible. The era of the lace and the monstrance being over, this no longer is true. The worldwide liturgical movement has pushed the "black" catholics out on the ritualistic limb. And they say that even at Pusey House the theologians are learning German. Scholarly works that are not merely restatements of Gore on the incarnation begin to appear. Fresh winds blow through the thoughts of our younger theologians; subjects other than the Elizabethan Settlement are found on theological agendas. While the bishops continue to compose position papers which seem somewhat sticky, there is no doubt that windows are being raised all over the house.

The second factor is the current Roman involvement in ecumenism—a movement that no longer bears the hallmarks of a pan-Protestant plot. Henry P. Van Dusen as the organization man of church unity is not now a threat. Here also a new freedom has appeared which manifests itself in a willingness to meet non-Anglicans face to face in those church councils and federations which most of us had considered crashing bores. We no longer like Baptists only at a distance; we are able to *talk* with them. And it grows upon us that they and others have important things to say.

The addition of the Roman (and not quite so esoteric Russian) ingredients to the ecumenical conversation has made it possible for a whole new body of Anglicans to join in without many of the serious reservations that once obtained. What lies ahead for the Episcopalians in this area is wide participation by these new, unselfconscious wings of catholic churchmen. This has important meanings for American ecumenical discussion. Up to this point the Episcopalians who have distinguished themselves in the movement toward unity have in the main been evangelicals. These are the men who maintained that union with the Presbyterians was eminently plausible because we all belonged to the same caste. They bore within themselves so little of the Anglican tension (William Temple's kind) that there was in fact little theologically

to distinguish them from their (then) liberal peers in Presbyterianism. They held an iron grip on the ecumenical movement,
and because this was so they conveyed to others a distorted image
of central Anglicanism. But their day is over. One says this, however, with a profound sense of gratitude for their single-eyed
focus on the goal of reunion.

At the same time the day of the extreme Anglo-catholic also
is over. When one hears the sweet voice of charity sing through
the counsels of many a Roman cardinal he has little patience for the
often vulgar and humiliating bigotries of transplanted tractarians.
But here again a valuable witness was made by the honest and
sensitive among the high churchmen. The "new" churchman owes
them much. And upon the ofttimes stormy tensions provided by
the clash of high with low, a new position is permitted to emerge;
a creation takes place upon which new tensions are erected. This
makes for lively change in the unchangeable mystery of the
church.

These familial squabbles often have amused the American non-
Anglican. The Roman participation in the ecumenical conversation may well help him to discover new dimensions in these issues,
and will also assist Anglicans in maintaining the dignity of some
of them. The sum of it is that most of the Christian world now
engaged in ecumenical activity is "catholic." The new Anglicans
thus engaged no longer believe that Reformation and post-Tri-
dentine red flags are forever the pennants of authentic Christian
battle. They will hope that in the conversations ahead the historically fixed polemical may be separated from that which is, so
to say, tradition-respected biblical. For them issues like that of
the "divided chancel" (a monastic monstrosity anyhow!) pale
in the presence of the revolutionary present.

As is the case with other worldwide communions, the Anglican
is beginning to discover itself. The effect of this on the Episcopal
Church cannot be underestimated. Far from reducing our interest
in the problems of wider Christian unity, it has served only to
intensify that concern. The reasons compelling African and Asian

Anglicans to search for paths to reunion, for example, are different and exciting. Rubbing shoulders with their theologies and strategies will revolutionize the mission philosophy of the American church. In many situations the truth now flows the other way and we sit at the feet of those brethren who live "overseas." We will begin, at last, to view the homeland ministry and mission in "missionary" frames of reference. We will not be so prone to blame the Russian church in its struggle with Soviet society when we review our own sad capitulation to American culture.

But more Episcopalians, clerical and lay, will begin to perceive the truth that to live as real Anglicans is to disappear as Anglicans. *It is the vocation of Anglicanism to die.* This has been the recurring motif in the thought of Stephen Bayne as Anglican executive officer, although one suspects a tongue in the episcopal cheek. In hard fact, the Anglican empire is being chipped away. South India was first, and others are to follow. We shall find increasing comfort in the words of Bishop Bloy of Los Angeles, who maintains that in this history of dissolution we are not losing daughters but gaining sons—the riches of a larger family life. As we die, how rich we shall become! What really lies ahead for us is the question of how we shall deal with our own death throes and the new life struggles that surely will follow.

III

As Anglicanism (and the Episcopal Church) becomes more aware of itself, the necessity of cutting the umbilical cord binding us to the mother Church of England becomes imperative. At the recent Anglican Congress in Toronto many American delegates were disturbed at the overpowering role played by Canterbury. Undoubtedly we and others within our communion will engage in delicate surgery in the days ahead. When one no longer feeds on the body of his mother he does not cast her out; he simply grows up. The difficulty is that the British talk better English, or at least they sound more profound. In any event the surgery will be difficult because our role in the Establishment in this country depends in part on this association with the mother in England. We are in the main white, Anglo-Saxon dependables. We serve the upper middle class and the classes even higher. As the dean of St. Paul's once observed, "The Prayer Book is meant for the literate."

The loving separation comes slowly. Recently a great seminary of our church produced a film to encourage contributions on that new day in the kalendar called Theological Education Sunday. Had the viewer missed the titles he would have surmised that here was a story out of England and its church. The motion picture in color depicted life in an enclosed theological school set in the midst of metropolis. The theological peak of the film showed a professor somewhat emotionally defending the glories of the Settlement in Elizabeth's reign. At the film's end its central character, the seminarian, now a rosy-cheeked young priest standing vested before a lily-bedecked altar, asks his well-dressed parishioners to lift up their suburban hearts.

The day comes, however, when we shall look at the industrial missions in Sheffield rather than at the ivy-colored walls of dead temples. We shall ponder in the new fashion of our metropolitans the strategies demanded in the Caribbean, in Africa and the East. We shall look to the sprawling metropolis and see there arising the new unity discerned by our increasing number of Gibson Winters. And in this meditation we shall feed not only on our Anglican heritage but also on those of the whole catholic Church of Christ.

IV

It really is urbanization that is tipping the scale in the Episcopal Church. A crisis always demands a response of some sort. Some of our prophets have warned us about it in the past; Dean Ladd was one, and today Niles Carpenter is another. Learning from him are the Fran Ayers, the Paul Moores, the Hugh Whites and a host of others—names new in the Episcopal Church so long dominated by aristocratic dynasties. Men like our primate, Arthur Lichtenberger (who sports the title "Most Reverend"), saw the handwriting on the wall; and to Episcopalians (save for a few klansmen in the deep south) our presiding bishop *is* the most. Under his gifted leadership the spirit of our central agency, the National Council, has changed so radically that even to visit its offices leads one to believe he is beholding a new church. Lichtenberger wears easily the cope and miter of the mysterious glue; he is grasped by the *mysterium* of the church. But he looks to our day and, along with all the sensitive, is racked by the imponderables of the future. He has brought into the council an impressive column from among our best clergy and laity. It is on these lines of leadership that directions are firming. The battle will be one with the culture; i. e., with those within our communion who remain embedded in the societal cement of a post-Christian age. And, at this writing, that means most Episcopalians.

Primary leadership can do only so much in the way of directing ministry and mission toward metropolis. It can, of course, bring powerful pressure to bear on the corporate structure of the church —the kind of pressure represented by socially and economically realistic John Heuss, rector of the Episcopal Church's greatest parish (Trinity, New York city), who believes that the church will be destroyed unless it sees the city as the frontier of mission. The additive necessary to engagement is the daringly unconventional which, while made tolerable by official direction, pushes forward to as yet untested experiences. This involves recognition of already existing ministries to metropolis outside the formal structure of the church and the fashioning of new ones inside the structure of the church. In the days to come Episcopalians will retool many existing ministries and create models of new ones. They know already that they cannot do this alone.

V

In Christian education circles the emphasis on the lay apostolate during the past several years will begin to bear fruit. In parish after parish one notes the lay response to the workings of the Spirit. The laity do not as yet know what to do with their freedom, but they are probing, and such probing is often the beginning of fruitful action. We are "between the times" in terms of knowing where this still tiny cadre will be led. Its movement no doubt will accelerate as more of our clergy join the church of silence. At the moment we must admit that few genuinely lay movements exist within the clericalized structure of the church. No doubt with us as with others it is too soon for daringly responsible lay leadership to emerge.

It may well be due to the mounting pressure of our William Stringfellows that the metropolitan church truly fitted to this age will appear. In this, if we may phantasize, one sees a constellation of truly "laos parishes" in which the people will come into their own. Their movement will be out into the metropolis where men and movements are to be found. The brick and mortar of the visible church, deemed so important now, will be reduced to a table with a roof over it. The priest will recover his rightful role as sacramental feeder of the flock of God, and many in this order will discover specialized theological ministries of teaching. These new priests will glory in their people who have become the cutting edge of the church in the world. And the bishop? He becomes the essential minister providing sacramental and historical continuity and speaking with authority the word of judgment.

One sees this dimly, but not as Anglicanism. It is rather the church beyond all particular confessions and yet informed by them all. As Chesterton wrote, in the church there are many mansions. It is the church suffering with contradictions and tensions but united in the *mysterium* of baptism and eucharist. The *mysterium* is as always mediated through a person rather than a committee. For most Christians in this world that *persona* is the bishop . . . who knew Irenaeus who knew Polycarp who knew John who saw the Lord.

Never before in the history of Anglicanism has there existed such openness to other Christians. This openness is coupled with an earnest desire to offer others only our tested strengths—and these unencumbered with our irrelevant prejudices. The entire movement of society—the whole revolutionary nature of it—has forced a new spirit upon this church. Its continued response to the challenges of the post-Christian world will depend on its willingness to listen humbly and with sensitive ears to the promptings of the Spirit.

15. PRESBYTERIANS, U.S.: ENROUTE TO BROADER CONCERNS

Aubrey N. Brown, Jr.*

Friends of southern Presbyterians (officially, the Presbyterian Church in the United States) who feel that this church is sometimes slow to bear its witness in significant ways or to take its full share in cooperative enterprises need to recognize a continuing internal struggle that exists within the denomination.

With nearly a million members in the seventeen traditionally southern states, plus a few congregations spilling over into New Mexico, Ohio and Pennsylvania, the church is not unaware of its position at the top of the annual stewardship statistics for denominations with more than 500,000 members, nor does it attempt to hide the number of its people who are influential in public affairs or who come from socially and economically privileged levels of the community. That such is the case may well be its condemnation.

It is not difficult to recognize how deeply involved this church was in the southern cause a century ago, not simply in its contribution of military personnel but also in the rationalization of the cause of the south by its founders, particularly by James H.

* Mr. Brown is editor of the *Presbyterian Outlook,* published in Richmond, Virginia, and serving both southern and northern Presbyterians.

Thornwell and Benjamin M. Palmer. These men and their associates were so powerful in stating the case that their continuing influence helps to explain some of the problems that persist to this day.

1

Four major problems, most if not all of them related to this dominant influence, have left their mark upon the church and its life: (1) the existence of its "distinctive" doctrine of the "spirituality of the church"; (2) the matter of relations with the larger Presbyterian, U.S.A., body from which it withdrew (now United Presbyterian, U.S.A.); (3) issues pertaining to the Negro; and (4) attitudes toward modern scholarship in relation to the Bible.

Presbyterian, U.S., insistence that the church is concerned only with "spiritual" affairs became a convenient device for escaping social responsibility. It actually led the church into a type of cultural captivity against which it has now been struggling for many years.

Southern Presbyterians have the same theological heritage as Congregationalists and northern (U.P.U.S.A.) Presbyterians, who have long been in the forefront of social concern and involvement. But the institution of slavery compelled the church in the south to justify its relation to that institution. It did so by turning away from the moral issue on the ground that such an issue was outside the church's province, that its chief obligation was spiritual—i.e., to evangelize and to make "good" Christians. Instead of looking critically at what was a heretical attack upon its traditional involvement in affairs of the common life, the leaders of the sectional church, in its formative years during the Civil War and during the subsequent and bitter reconstruction, proudly supported this thesis as the distinctive doctrine which justified its separate existence.[1]

[1] This thesis is developed in detail in Ernest Trice Thompson's *The Spirituality of the Church*, John Knox Press, 1961.

There are many evidences that this doctrine remains an obstacle to the church's witness. Denominational representatives in the National Council of Churches achieved the dubious distinction of being the only denominational group in the council to publicize their unwillingness to support the notable August 28 March on Washington. They made it clear that they were in basic sympathy with the hopes of the marchers and that they are seeking in their own way to achieve a desegregated society, but that they did not think the church should bless or encourage the demonstrations and, particularly, that they were sure their rank-and-file members would not support such action. They were afraid that continuing attacks on the council might be stepped up and that those who are committed to the doctrine of the "spirituality of the church" would make new efforts to pull the church out of the orbit of Protestant cooperation. That the group of such critics is continually dwindling and that generations of ministers have shown themselves committed to the church's best traditions of concern and involvement did not seem to be enough to offset the threat the representatives sensed.

Some observers appraised the 1963 General Assembly as one of the best in terms of advance steps taken: the most far-reaching and urgent admonition on race relations yet recorded, overwhelming rejection of those who would attempt to press the church into narrower molds, approval of the ordination of women and submission of that issue to the presbyteries for ratification, strong support voted for the National Council along with stiff-arm rejection of its critics, expression of the "ultimate" conviction that "the Presbyterian and Reformed communions of the United States should present a united life and witness." Still, in his comments on that assembly in the *Presbyterian Outlook*, Kenneth J. Foreman called attention to the "silences" of the assembly: nothing said about riots and racial disturbances then in evidence, nothing said about the Bomb, rejection of an effort to consider the tobacco issue, inadequate treatment of freedom of utterance in the church and "mighty little self-criticism; few calls for repentance." The old doctrine of the "spirituality of the church" holds on, though its hold is gradually relaxing.

II

The denomination's attempt to celebrate its 100th anniversary in 1961 was an inglorious failure, reflecting again a deep division in the church's life. The celebration aroused no enthusiasm because of the commonly expressed opinion that it is not proper to celebrate a divorce. Members who are concerned for reunion of the American Presbyterian family are constantly challenged by the question of how the church can honestly call its people to meet the reconciling terms of the gospel if it is not willing to reunite with its northern brethren.

The latest movement toward such union, ten years ago, could hardly have succeeded even without the fever heat generated by the Supreme Court's desegregation ruling. Since 1913 proposals for union have required a favorable vote in three-fourths of the presbyteries, and that kind of approval cannot be gained on any issue which generates significant tensions. Although the 1962 assembly expressed "ultimate hope" of American Presbyterian reunion, many feel that there is little hope for negotiations with the northern branch so long as that church remains involved in the Consultation on Church Union under the inspiration of the Blake proposal.

Today union is being talked and plans are being made looking toward possible merger with the Reformed Church in America, which is about one-fourth the size of the Presbyterian Church, U.S. There appears to be strong southern Presbyterian support for such union, though some qualms and questions are raised. It is not clear what this step would do to comity with the United Presbyterian Church, U.S.A., nor whether it would retard or speed up possible union with that church. Members and leaders of the Presbyterian Church, U.S., and the Reformed Church in America have few points of contact; they know very little about each other, and a gap of hundreds of miles separates most of them geographically. There are indications, however, that in the R.C.A., fundamentalist groups and more liberal-spirited leaders will have to come to terms in their own ranks before Presbyterians actually face a genuine choice in the matter of union.

Although it has been sectional and apart from much of the nation's life, the Presbyterian Church, U.S., has supported co-operative enterprises since the launching of the World Presbyterian Alliance in 1875. It remains in the National and World councils despite repeated attacks on those bodies by some of its constituents. (When the number of its members criticizing the old Federal Council became great enough to compel its withdrawal from 1932 to 1940, *The Christian Century* said, in effect if not in words: Good riddance; if they are going to drag their heels all the time it is better for them to be out.) The pro-cooperation majority continues to grow and, even though attacks on cooperation have not ceased, it appears that the church will maintain and strengthen its ecumenical concern and allegiance.

III

When the National Council representatives took their stand on the Washington March, one southern Presbyterian theological candidate serving an internship in New York state wrote: "The image which is widely held in the north (falsely, I believe) that the Presbyterian Church, U.S., is a little southern Zion concerned with fundamentalism and segregation, was strengthened by this "action." Let us look first at the latter concern, then at the former.

The southern Presbyterian Church has only a small Negro membership, far smaller than 100 years ago, but in many ways the denomination appears to be doing more toward desegregation in its own body than are several, if not most, other predominantly white denominations working in the south. Its separate and seg-regated synod for Negro ministers and churches was dissolved nearly twenty years ago, and even such separate presbyteries as exist are passing out with an increasing number of Negro churches coming into otherwise white presbyteries. In most situations newly organized Negro churches become a part of the presbytery in whose bounds they are located; all across the church, camps, conferences, leadership schools and all facilities are open to both races without restriction. The seminaries opened their doors years ago, and today all but a few of the church's colleges have come into line with the General Assembly's summons to integrate. The assembly and most of its agencies have made it a matter of policy that they will not meet where all their members cannot be treated alike. There are a few integrated churches, and increasing numbers are declaring their willingness to receive Negro members. All this is far from enough, and the movement is slow—but it is movement in the right direction, and there will be no retreat.

IV

Negative actions like that in regard to the Washington March get publicity while more positive steps in the direction of theological concern and intellectual freedom receive less attention, but it has been a good while since a genuine attempt at heresy-hunting was made in the Presbyterian Church, U.S., and far longer since one succeeded.

When an all-out attack was made last year on the *Layman's Bible Commentary* issued by the denominational publishers, the General Assembly routed the attackers and gave to the commentary, modern scholarship and intellectual freedom better than a 6-1 vote of confidence. Pockets of fundamentalists may cause some trouble as they do in churches elsewhere in the nation, but they cannot determine denominational policies. Even in the synod of Mississippi there is an alert watchfulness against infiltration by ministers who want to get into the church to bend it in the direction of fundamentalist objectives. A few years ago that synod issued a warning to its constituents to be alert to the danger of receiving men from fundamentalist denominations centered largely in the north.

Some months ago a symposium of theological professors looked at the issue of biblical infallibility; these men, one from each of the four seminaries, made it clear that the fundamentalist position is untenable and that the findings of modern scholarship must be followed. Here and there troubled voices were raised against the position they took—but not many, and in no case did a scholar of standing in the church attack their conclusions.

In the discussion of the ordination of women now going on among southern Presbyterians, the biblical and theological leadership of the church has almost without exception made it clear that old lines of biblical interpretation are unsound. What happens in the next few months while presbyteries are deciding whether to reject or ratify the General Assembly's approval of the ordination of women will reveal much about the maturity of the church. How they meet the issue will not only indicate something of its sociological orientation but, more important, it will show whether what most scholars consider to be an invalid use of the Bible is determinative in the life of the church. The vote of the first 37 of the 80 presbyteries showed a majority of 23-14 in favor. In 1957 the proposal lost 44-39. A simple majority is required.[2]

In this field the seminaries stand together, and they are condemned together by fundamentalist forces whose aim is to have southern Presbyterian ministerial candidates go to some alien institution where they will be taught that this church and its leadership are unsound and not to be trusted. Such ultraconservative critics have long been unhappy about the direction in which the church's leadership and educational institutions are moving. They have tried in many ways to stem the tide, but they will admit that they are not hopeful that they can to any degree bring about a return to the dominant position which they occupied thirty to forty years ago when they could control policies.

---

[2] In the event, the vote was approved by the presbyteries 53-27 and was enacted into the law of the church by the 1964 General Assembly.

Now about all they can hope for is to raise voices of protest, to attempt to frighten leaders and to keep them back from the frontier.

V

This largely middle-class church recognizes that there are few poor people on its rolls, and that many of its members do not even know any poor people. In many communities the working class is not represented, and the church has scant touch with organized labor. The fact that men associated with management and ownership are dominant in the church's membership may explain but does not justify the fact that even General Assembly committees charged with probing social responsibility have not yet dealt with the issue of labor-management relations. The church's recent annual Christian Action Conference did indeed look at labor-management issues, but in that conference there was scant if any labor representation from within the church.

Leadership of the Presbyterian, U.S., boards and agencies is generally informed, ecumenical and progressive. However, problems are inevitably posed by the fact that planning must be regional instead of nationwide; the church has paid a high price for its 100 years of division. It is difficult for a regional body to think and plan in big categories, and to have the benefit of balancing and corrective points of view such as come from areas subjected to other pressures and cultural influences. But today heartening signs of a change in emphasis are discernible.

The Board of World Missions, which has not always led the way in Protestant cooperation, last year sponsored a unique consultation which enlisted enthusiastic participation, frank criticism and re-evaluation of policies and programs, with nationals from around the world and leaders from other mission boards pooling their ideas along with missionaries and homefolks. Results of the consultation are already shattering the molds of generations; the future tone and policies of this board will probably help move

the church on to a new level. Meanwhile, approximately $3 million
and years of effort have produced the new Covenant Life Curriculum, which offers comprehensive educational direction to the
entire constituency. This project has attracted the interest of many
Protestant leaders and won their favorable approval. Depending
on what happens with the teaching materials at the point of local
contact—how effectively teachers use them and how capable the
teachers are—the project can have a far-reaching influence.

VI

Any really critical look at what has traditionally been regarded as evangelism is equated by some southern Presbyterians
with tampering with the sacred ark. But many others agree that
the old patterns are ineffective; they insist that in any informed
approach to the existing culture, old clichés and superficial
analyses of the past are worthless. Yet when questions are raised
by pioneering leaders in regard to existing structures some people
are shocked and impelled to clamor for investigation of the background of the leadership.

Plenty of southern Presbyterians—including an occasional official—would be satisfied to keep on doing the same old things but
doing more of them and doing them better: erecting more and
bigger church buildings, holding more meetings and more conferences, acquiring more members and more money. But there
are many others who know that this kind of frenzied effort can
indicate guilt or escape rather than spiritual health and spiritual
motivation. Everybody was gratified that in response to a $12-
million capital needs campaign, the church came forth with more
than $15.5 million. But this kind of response is far easier and
much less costly than challenging the local power structure to
come to grips with issues having to do with justice, or achieving
a church that is genuinely integrated and concerned, or planning
wisely and projecting effectively a congregational program that

meets the basic needs of people in the places where they live and work.

In their local communities, southern Presbyterians will always be found in the van of cooperative ventures; they will work gladly with the people they know and they will pay their share of the bill. But only time will tell whether they can adjust to the increasing shift from rural to urban living situations, whether they can help the economically privileged come to terms with the demands upon them, whether they can deal with the cult of ecclesiastical administrative and promotional success which minimizes the theological task and the prophetic witness, and whether they will be left as an ecclesiastical backwater in the stream of the larger ecumenical current. In the church's unsettled life there is enough ferment and discontent to encourage its members—and its well-wishers—to view the future with hope.

16. AMERICAN LUTHERANISM: DENOMINATION OR CONFESSION?

Jaroslav Pelikan*

One of my favorite theological parlor games is to ask a student or a churchman: "Which denomination would you join if your own were suddenly to collapse or if it were finally to decide that you are *persona non grata?*" During the ten years that I have been teaching historical theology in interdenominational divinity schools, I have received some highly revealing and some quite bizarre reactions to my question; but even when I was a professor at a confessional seminary I used to get extremely diverse answers,

* Dr. Pelikan is Titus Street professor of ecclesiastical history at Yale Divinity School.

answers that are perhaps symptomatic of the inner ambiguities of Lutheranism in America. There is an implicit answer to the question and an explicit proof for the ambiguities in these random facts from the history of American Lutheranism: "Old Swedes' Church" was Lutheran but became Episcopalian; Walter A. Maier, the best-known radio evangelist of this century, at least before Billy Graham, was a Lutheran; the attitude of some Lutherans toward the Bible is indistinguishable from that of fundamentalism. Thus this Lutheran version of "What's Ahead for the Churches?" could consist of a recital of the several confessional options toward which American Lutheranism seems to be moving and of an assessment of relative desirability and the likelihood of their adoption.

But that would be begging the question, for historically at least, this foliation of theological diversity within some sort of confessional unity is closer to the tradition of Lutheranism than is the identification of confessional unity with uniformity that many Lutherans in this country would regard as normative. To an extent not always recognized by either insiders or outsiders, Lutheran history in America has been dominated not only by the ethnic flavor of a denomination almost completely Nordic in stock, but by a Pietism that could be either confessionally rigid or confessionally indifferent without surrendering its distinctive character. Thus the orthodoxy of C. F. W. Walther, founder of the Missouri Synod, and the evangelicalism of S. S. Schmucker, exponent of "American Lutheranism," actually shared with each other a form of religious experience and emphasis that has continued to appear in their descendants. Although he warned against the religious exercises of the Pietists as a "mingling of Law and Gospel," Walther's own preaching and ethical teaching showed unmistakable traces of his apprenticeship under Pietists. What Walther wrote about dancing and the ethics of sex and what Schmucker taught about drinking proved how much of the Pietist heritage they shared after all.

Significantly, they shared it with a large part of the rest of

American Protestantism, so that the process of Americanization
frequently came to mean the strengthening of the Pietist heritage
brought over from the Old World. (As a matter of fact, the
coalescence of Puritanism and Pietism in the several Protestant
traditions is one of the most important and most neglected lines
of inquiry in American church history.) Therefore an observer
who has known Lutheranism chiefly in its European expression
or in the generalizations of Ernest Troeltsch and Karl Barth will
be astonished to discover how thoroughly Puritan and theocratic
it can become in America; indeed, it was a Lutheran minister, now
a member of the House of Representatives, who introduced the
"Christian amendment to the Constitution" in the Congress! The
"Evangelical Alliance" at the middle of the nineteenth century
was both a cause and an effect of this confluence of Pietistic and
Puritan elements. It seems fairly predictable that American Lutheranism will continue to adapt itself ever more completely to
its American Protestant environment during the next decades, and
that, for better or for worse, it will become a denomination.

Most likely, it will be both for better and for worse. The
American experience has enriched Lutheran thought and life in
many ways and will certainly go on doing so. Lutheran preaching in America has discovered a social concern it did not have
when it came over, at last beginning to break with the political
conservatism of its European past. Lutheran theology has been
compelled to come to terms with some philosophers besides
Kant, although it still finds Kierkegaard easier to deal with than
Thomas Aquinas. Lutherans have sometimes exchanged their
birthright of hymnody for a mess of gospel songs, as the earliest
English hymnals and "Sunday School hymnals" demonstrate; but
from many sources they have also learned hymns that have permanently deepened their piety and worship. The mass media have
opened their microphones and cameras to Lutheran programs—
or, at least, to programs by Lutherans, since Lutheran programs
on radio and television have generally done a better job of docu-
menting what is Protestant about Lutheranism than of manifest-

ing what is Catholic about it. Above all, Lutherans have begun
to learn in the United States that the only base broad enough to
support their confessional loyalty and to rescue it from sectarian
debasement is an ecumenically aroused Christendom. A church
that seeks to save its life shall lose it, but a church that is willing,
for the sake of its Lord, to invest itself in the total life of the
total church will receive its own life back. Whatever is worth
salvaging from the Lutheran tradition ought to be tough enough
to survive in an interdenominational milieu. We have nothing to
lose but our isolation.

Whatever else we may lose that we ought to keep, will be lost
because, despite the bravado, the Lutheran Church in America
has been drinking from cisterns it did not dig. It has kept the
ecumenical creeds in its worship and its dogmatics, but a uni-
tarianism of the Second Person has become the working theology
of many of its preachers and people. Jesus Christ appears as the
object of worship, the addressee of prayer, and the source of
comfort, without explicit reference to the Father and the Holy
Spirit. "Come to Jesus" is a standard evangelistic appeal. It can,
of course, claim biblical precedent, as can prayer addressed to
Christ. But in the liturgy of the Christian tradition, such prayer
is the exception; the rule is prayer to the Father through the
Son for the help of the Holy Spirit. Subtle though the shift may
seem from authentic Trinitarianism to such Christocentric Uni-
tarianism, it is no less profound or important.

Similarly, Lutheranism in America still teaches the real presence
and may still bar from the communion rail those whose definition
of the real presence it regards as erroneous or inadequate; but in
most places it has the opportunity to bar them only once a month,
since this supposedly liturgical church, which criticized the
church of the Middle Ages for neglecting frequency of communion, is still a long way from a weekly celebration of the
Lord's Supper. As I can testify from frequent personal experience
in most parts of the United States and Canada, there are many
large cities and "Lutheran centers" in which, on a given Sunday,
it is impossible for a Lutheran to communicate in a Lutheran

church. One parish of my acquaintance inaugurated a weekly celebration at 10:00 A.M., between an early and a late preaching service without communion. One Sunday, as I was leaving after the celebration, I was asked by a puzzled parishioner: "Aren't you staying for church?" It is ironic that the dichotomy between the visible and the invisible church has sometimes enabled Lutheran churchmen to rationalize their separatism on the grounds that only the invisible church needs to be one, but this same dichotomy has not prevented them from advancing the cause of their own ecclesiastical organizations as though the visible and the invisible church were coextensive. At least a confessional isolationism kept its contact with the fathers, if not with the brethren, but this new denominationalism runs the risk of following the most shallow contemporary fads in the Church even while it still stands off reciting its formulas of discord.

Perhaps the most damaging feature of such denominationalism is that the reaction which it will inevitably call forth may drain away not only Lutheran isolation but Lutheran theological vitality as well. Trying to predict whether or not it will is made difficult by the Lutheran habit of imitating Martha while it praises Mary. Thus at one convention some years ago, hours were spent debating whether the most recent in a long series of doctrinal agreements aiming at Lutheran unity was explicit enough in ruling out any action on a man's part before conversion; the same convention endorsed a multi-million-dollar financial drive with a "whereas" which claimed that all over the world millions of souls were "pleading" for the gospel. We launched our edition of *Luther's Works* when we did at least partly out of the feeling that this might be the last generation within American Lutheranism that could mount the resources needed for the task. Yet the enthusiastic response to the edition, which goes well beyond mere patriotism, and the use being made of it give ground for the hope that the next generation of Lutherans in America may, even without German or Latin, discover more of the authentic heritage of the Reformation than its fathers knew.

If this hope is fulfilled, a considerable share of the credit will have to go not only to the seminaries, but to the Lutheran colleges and universities. The next two or three decades may tell the story one way or the other about Lutheran schools in the United States. It is, of course, true that some Lutheran colleges are already indistinguishable from their secularized, post-Protestant neighbors and that others are academically and intellectually mediocre. But it is also true that some Lutheran colleges have become centers for a theological and intellectual life of a very high order, with a responsibility not only for correlating the Christian faith with the academic disciplines, but also for the basic research in theology that has traditionally been reserved for the seminaries. At the Lutheran university with which I am most familiar, Valparaiso University, a large and vigorous department of theology has been engaged in historical, biblical, and philosophical investigations and discussions significant enough to attract nationwide attention from both Roman Catholics and Protestants and to stir up some thunder on the right. To wait for theological insights to "trickle down" to the laity would be too leisurely a strategy in the present state of the intellectual and spiritual life of American Lutheranism; therefore theological renewal must involve lay education immediately, and for this prospect there are some truly encouraging signs.

Equally encouraging is the liturgical renewal. Like every other denomination, American Lutheranism has had its share of precious aesthetes and ritualists, and perhaps more than its share. But these must not be confused with the virile and creative minds who have been working for the revival of worship and the arts. Certainly the most dramatic expression of this revival is church architecture during the past decade and a half, beginning perhaps with Christ Church in Minneapolis by Saarinen *père et fils* in 1950. Gimmicks there have been, and outlandish mistakes as well, but if the churches constructed in the next twenty-five years are just as experimental but more functionally related to Lutheran worship and teaching, this could be an exciting time for both architects and parishes. The same period will probably witness a

greater willingness to draw the implications of the priesthood
of believers for the liturgy with at least as much boldness and
radicalism as some Roman Catholics have shown. In such buildings, with such experimentation, the worshiping congregation
can really be involved in the action of the liturgy, so that liturgy
does not become (as I heard one layman define it) "What the
pastor does between hymns." Most of all, this liturgical renewal
should pay attention to the often overlooked but nevertheless
fundamental emphasis of confessional Lutheranism on the connection between Word and sacrament, urging the churches toward
a worship that is truly eucharistic and toward a preaching that is
truly biblical.

To be truly biblical, however, Lutheran preaching will need
to acquire some biblical accents that it has lost in the past few
years or has not had for a long time. As a textual preacher who
now listens far oftener than he preaches, I have repeatedly been
shocked to see how thin a scriptural veneer covers the hortatory
moralism and alien sentimentality of much Lutheran preaching. It
has been noted by Heinrich Bornkamm of Heidelberg that if
Martin Luther were to be a member of a modern theological
faculty, he would be professor not of systematic theology nor
even of New Testament, but of Old Testament. Even when he
dealt with the New Testament, he approached it as one who was
saturated with the language and imagery of the Old Testament—
just as the writers of the New Testament were themselves. Therefore one change I hope for is the rediscovery of the Old Testament
in the Lutheran pulpit. From such a rediscovery could also come,
as it has so often in the history of the church, a passion for social
justice and a dedication to the purposes of God for all humanity.
Lutheran theology and Lutheran preaching alike have tended to
oscillate between antinomianism and legalism, both of which can
be offset, not by further refinement of traditional Lutheran no-
tions about Law and Gospel, but by a radical reappropriation
of the full range of biblical speech and thought—not merely that
of Romans and Galatians. Yet Lutherans go on writing com-

mentaries on these two epistles, as though there were no apostles but Paul, or as though Paul had written no other epistles but these, or as though the concern of the apostle Paul had been identical with Luther's. Whatever may come of the highly publicized "new quest for the historical Jesus" generally, a church that still tells its people to rise for the reading of the lesson from the gospels would do well to ask whether its proclamation and life have been sufficiently informed by the message of the gospels. As Lutheran preaching finds itself less and less able to presuppose even rudimentary biblical acquaintance (not to say catechetical preparation) among its hearers, it will have to become more sophisticated and yet more naive about the Bible.

Just such a combination of sophistication and naivete characterized Luther's own use of the Bible. Now that his commentaries on the Bible are becoming available in English, Lutherans are beginning to see both the power of his biblical thought and the impossibility of simply repeating it today. Perhaps only Origen and Augustine have covered the depth and breadth of the Bible as thoroughly as Martin Luther; yet the very power in the exegesis of all three that still grips us also dramatizes the unbridgeable distance between them and us. The deepening commitment of American Lutheranism to the ecumenical movement is having many effects upon its thought, but none is more interesting than the discovery that outside of American Lutheranism, which has not produced more than a handful of creative biblical scholars in its entire history, men in other traditions have been penetrating to the meaning of Scripture in a way that is both faithful to the text and open to modern thought, in other words, in a way that thus parallels Luther's own expository method without repeating it. And "other traditions" means not only European Lutheranism and American Protestantism, but also (and increasingly) Roman Catholicism, to which, it seems to me, Lutherans have a special responsibility and responsiveness. It would be a tragic mistake if American Lutheranism were to regard itself as simply a part of Protestantism in relation to the Roman Catholic

Church; for in many notable ways the Lutheran combination of
"Catholic substance and Protestant principle" makes the situation
of Lutheranism more complex and more difficult than that of
other churches. During the next two decades, I am confident,
Lutheranism in the United States will find that the only hope for
its own biblical and confessional integrity is an ecumenical involvement with other heirs of the Reformation and with "the
separated brethren of the Latin obedience."

For Lutheranism cannot escape the vicious dilemma of denominationalism versus interdenominationalism unless it finds a
way of being authentically confessional, that is, simultaneously
more Catholic and more Reformed than it is now. If it settles
for Lutheran unity, clutches its confessions desperately to its
breast, and turns away from its Roman Catholic and its Protestant
brethren, it will lose both Catholic substance and Protestant principle. But in the opportunities created by the emergence of new
life in Roman Catholicism and in Protestantism, Lutheranism
stands a chance of finding the new life and unity it needs and thus
of reinterpreting both Catholic substance and Protestant principle. It is my hope and earnest prayer that it will recognize that
chance and will take it, in faithful obedience to its Lord and in
fraternal concord with all who name the name of Christ.

17. THE CHURCHES AND THE WORLD

Kyle Haselden*

Attempts to forecast the future of the churches are reliable to
the extent that they rise, not from abstract speculations, but from
a careful diagnosis of the present status of the churches. My con-

* Kyle Haselden is Editor of *The Christian Century*.

tribution to the predictions in this volume pictures in broad
strokes the present encounter of church and social problems and,
by conjectures based on the current situation, describes the direction in which the relationship of the churches and the social problems will move in the years ahead. The province of my concern
encompasses not one denomination but all of the churches. (To
avoid awkwardness I use Christian terms even where the generalities of this article include Judaism.) By "social issues" I mean
the racial problem, poverty, health and welfare, church-state tensions, political radicalism in its various forms, the capital-manage-
ment-labor controversies, automation and unemployment. My
purpose excludes detailed descriptions of particular problems and
specific counseling of the churches in their denominational approach or lack of approach to the problems. What is the present,
collective impact of the churches and the social issues upon each
other? What turns will that relationship take in the future? These
are the questions which this chapter of "What's Ahead for the
Churches?" seeks to answer.

Even a brief analysis of the social activity of the churches should
note first that the Social Gospel as an American ecclesiastical
movement and as a formalized church party has been dead in the
churches for more than a generation. Never widely accepted, this
particularly American brand of social Christianity died prema-
turely, leaving behind much unfinished business and few heirs.
With all due credit to him, we must see Walter Rauschenbusch,
not as the pioneer of the Social Gospel movement, but as the
towering terminal figure—and a somewhat tragic figure—in a
long succession which began in mid-19th century America and
which numbered such men as William Ellery Channing, Lyman
Abbott, Washington Gladden, Stephen Colwell, Richard Ely,
Josiah Strong, Horace Bushnell and others. Beyond the peak
reached in Rauschenbusch the Social Gospel, dedicated to the
redemption of society and confident that this redemption could
be brought off, dissolved before internal weaknesses and external
assaults with which it was unable to cope. As a proper name the

phrase "Social Gospel" remains only as an historical phenomenon. In part the death of the Social Gospel was suicidal. On at least three counts the movement must be charged with its own destruction, and its failures as well as its successes should guide social Christianity in the future. First, the Social Gospel was weakened internally by the narrowness of its concern. It concentrated almost exclusively on economic problems and slighted the equally crucial problems of war, race, imperialism. Rauschenbusch's *Christianizing the Social Order* might just as accurately have been entitled *Christianizing the Economic Order*. Horace Bushnell and Josiah Strong not only ignored the racial problem in their writings but also displayed glaring evidences of racial pride. Social justice for George D. Herron meant almost exclusively a revolutionizing of the economic base of society; most Social Gospel proponents followed this lead. When this concern was eventually absorbed by the political order under liberal governments the Social Gospel lost its primary reason for being and collapsed. In one sense it won the economic battle, but it lost the sociological war within the churches.

Second, the Social Gospel withered from the lack of theological grounding and nourishment, not because no such stabilizing and fertilizing soil was available to it but because Social Gospel pioneers did not, until too late, see the need for a biblically and doctrinally rooted social Christianity. To be sure, George D. Herron wrote in 1891: "It is moral superficialness to decry the study of theology. There can be no social system not based upon theological conceptions." Nevertheless the Social Gospel did decry theology. James Dombrowski pointed out that "Social Christianity, as it emerged into the proportions of a movement in the last two decades of the nineteenth century, had a decidedly antitheological bias." Years later Walter Rauschenbusch tried to correct this deficiency with his *A Theology for the Social Gospel*, but the remedy came too late and was inadequate. Building an ethical structure in the air and trying to put a theological substructure under it later always fails. When theology came once more into its own a social program which had rejected theology and which had no theological underpinnings could no longer stand.

Third, some of the Social Gospel pioneers allowed their movement to become too closely identified with Marxist principles. By occasionally echoing Marxist prescriptions as well as sometimes accurate Marxist diagnoses of the social evils, the Social Gospel prophets exposed their program to attacks by the fundamentalist wing of the churches and by blocs of reactionary businessmen. The dependence of some Social Gospel prophets upon Marxist analysis was not merely a tactical mistake, not merely a blunder which made the movement vulnerable to assaults by the American right wing. Even more it was a theoretical and philosophical error. Both in analysis and prescription Marxism makes a bad ally for social Christianity not because it is alien to our culture and to our political and social traditions but because it is false—an erroneous reading of the nature of man, a myopic view of history, and in addition an impractical economy. For these reasons, to say nothing of Marxism's basic atheism, the Social Gospel prophets should have made their rejection of Marxist aims and means unequivocal.

Social Christianity in mid-20th century should not hanker for the return of a system which professed the perfectibility of man and of his social structures, which glossed over the intricacy of human nature and the complexity of society, which sought the fulfillment of human history within human history and which ignored the fact that man sins as readily in Eden as out of it. But it must mourn the demise of that social concern and social commitment which informed and motivated the Social Gospel. However circuitous the line may be, there is a connection between yesterday's church which—usually for the wrong reasons —feared, distrusted and grew tired of its social prophets and today's church which in the main has come to terms with society at the expense of its gospel. The gospel which claims the whole realm of being and proclaims Christ as imperial and universal

Lord has been reduced in its sphere to man's interior life and
in its authority to the Christian community.

Despite the belated and still partial waking of white Christian
churches to their duty in the current racial struggles, despite
the noble social resolutions and directives adapted and issued by
the denominations from the top down, despite the existence of
committees and boards on Christian life and Christian social concern, despite such courageous social documents as *Pacem in Terris*
and *Mater et Magistra*, social ethics is still largely rejected by the
churches as a term, a challenge and an obligation. Ironically, as
the churches become more and more secularized, they become
less and less effective and decreasingly acceptable as guardians of
the social order. This says, in other words, that society has tamed
the churches. In a tragic reversal of the church's early history, the
world has turned the churches upside down. The province
of the church's influence and authority has steadily decreased
even while in a demographic sense the scope of the church has
increased. The churches and the spheres of man's secular life circle
like marbles in a jar, touching each other but not penetrating.
The churches bump against the world, but they leave few marks
on it.

An even more dismaying fact than the isolation of the churches
from the pitiless realities of contemporary history and their withdrawal from the world is the ignorance or indifference of the
average churchman to what is happening to the churches as they
default their duty to the world. What happens when the gospel
is retracted from all contact with the world is bad for the world,
but it is also bad for the gospel. In a background paper for the
World Council of Churches department on church and society
J. M. Lochmann wrote that "the clear message of Jesus is illumined
for us afresh [when] we take the new situation seriously. It is
not the historical events themselves which give his message this
additional force. Nothing in history could ever do that. But Jesus'
commandment, which has been watered down into abstract terms,
becomes strong and powerful when we obediently apply the

Gospel to actual life. This is another reason why the historical situation must be taken seriously." The fault is not that the average churchman, lay and clerical, does not take history and the world seriously but that he does not take history and the world seriously in the light of the gospel, nor does he take the gospel seriously in the light of history and the world. The result is an abandoned world, a misdirected history and an atrophied gospel. The more the gospel is withdrawn from the world—whether by the church, to cloister and protect the gospel, or by an autocratic world, to free itself from all moral tethers—the more certainly and swiftly does the gospel wither and lose its vitality. The gospel does not, like the mythological Greek giant, Antaeus, get its strength from the earth, but its strength is released and renewed as it touches man in all his circumstances. By drawing a *cordon sanitaire* between the gospel and society the churchman abandons the world and dooms the gospel. The churches were not called into being to rule the world but to serve it, not to reject the world but to embrace it with a redeeming love, not to withdraw from the world but to penetrate it with a healing and nurturing spirit. When churchmen deny their churches this role they are in fact denying their Lord's sovereignty over the whole man. And this is what they do when, ignorant or misguided, they reject social Christianity or, if Jews, make their religion a sanctuary into which they retreat from the blows of a hostile world.

No one reading this book can doubt the detachment of the churches from the major social problems facing man in this generation. In several of the chapters there is little or no reference to war, race, poverty, political and social obscurantism, or even to such traditionally denounced social ills as alcoholism, prostitution and gambling. This deficiency is not due to poor scholarship on the part of the authors but to the absence of demonstrated social concern in the church. True, during the year in which these essays were written some of the churches began to awake to the challenge of racial discrimination and segregation. This, in part,

accounts for the priority given to the racial problem in this
study's scant references to social issues. It will be an interesting phenomenon if the pendulum of social Christianity swings
from an almost total disregard for the plight of the Negro to a
preoccupation with the Negro's problems. The racial problem,
the most pressing social issue of the century, tempts the soul of
the churches as nothing else does. Nevertheless it will be ironic
if the churches permit a growing awareness of, and response to,
the racial challenge to preempt their social sensitiveness and activity, thus repeating one of the Social Gospel's fatal errors.

Samuel H. Hill, Jr.'s reference to "vexing problems" in his
chapter on the Southern Baptist Convention illustrates the paucity
of social commitment in that denomination as in others, for the
"vexing problems" are in this case the church's identity with its
society, its absorption by its culture. The Southern Baptist Convention's Christian Life Commission strives valiantly and often
daringly to jar that church awake to its duty to man in all the
broad currents of his life. The Southern Baptist Convention's
toleration of such goading by an agency completely under its control is a glimmer of hope in a denomination which still slumbers
in the midst of a great social conflict and upheaval. What Samuel
H. Hill, Jr., wrote of his church applies to others. In them "the
Christian message bypasses the great personal and social ills of
our day to concentrate wholly or primarily on one's status before
a judgmental God in the life to come. . . ."

At least two churchmen contributing to this series flatly
denounced the ethical indifference and ineffectiveness of the
churches. In his analysis of peace churches J. Lawrence Burkholder writes of churches in general: "The practical failure of
typical congregations in America—including those of the peace
churches—to decide and to act corporately is one of the clues
to the ethical blandness of Protestantism. Most churches simply
do not know how to come to conclusions about things that matter.
Nor do they see decision-making as one of the marks of the
church." Aubrey N. Brown is similarly forthright in his analysis

of the social paralysis in his denomination in a specific area: "The fact that men associated with management and ownership are dominant in the church's membership may explain but does not justify the fact that even General Assembly committees charged with probing social responsibility have not yet dealt with the issue of labor-management relations."

The Episcopal and the Roman Catholic churchmen view the involvement of their churches in man's social needs critically but optimistically. C. Kilmer Myers sees his Episcopal church exchanging traditionalism for encounter: "The day comes, however, when we shall look at the industrial missions in Sheffield rather than at the ivy-covered walls of dead temples. We shall ponder in the new fashion of our metropolitans the strategies demanded in the Caribbean, in Africa and the East. We shall look to the sprawling metropolis and see there arising the new unity discerned by our increasing number of Gibson Winters. And in this meditation we shall feed not only on our Anglican heritage but also on those of the whole catholic Church of Christ." Bernard Cooke, S. J., believes that the increasing prominence of the lay Roman Catholic "gives clear promise of a greater involvement of the Catholic community in American social, political and cultural life." To this Protestants would have to answer that the involvement of the laity in Protestant church life has had, as Aubrey N. Brown confessed, a contrary effect. Lay control over the involvement of the church in social and political problems and the application of the church's teachings to those problems has tended to restrain rather than liberate the social message of the churches.

Thus these essays give us three perspectives of the relationship of the churches to the social issues. Some of the chapters ignore the social problems simply because the churches they represent ignore the problems. Some of the chapters forthrightly condemn the dereliction of the churches in translating their aspirations and resolutions into actions. And some of the chapters look wistfully toward the day when the churches they portray will obey their Lord's orders by taking up the burdens of the world. From each

perspective the church's glaring deficiency appears to be a preoccupation with itself and with the internal life of its members
and an indifferent or prudential withdrawal from those arenas
in which men collide, struggle and die. From all angles the picture
is dismaying. However hopefully and trustingly we may look to
the God of history to work out his will in the affairs of men,
little in the current life of the church encourages belief that the
church will be the instrument through which God will achieve
his purposes with men in the world.

To explain why the church has become in our day both a
secularized institution and an inept religious enclave isolated from
the social struggles churning around it would require more probing of the past than this prediction of the future permits. It is
well, however, to have in mind several generalities as we anticipate
the interplay of the churches and the social issues in the years
immediately ahead: First, Christians have tended to view "the
world" which "God so loved" and into which the risen Christ
sent his disciples, in geographic rather than in sociological terms.
This view has fostered foreign missions while simultaneously dis-
couraging social action. The misguided concern of the churches
has been dedicated to covering rather than penetrating the world
with the gospel. No church illustrates the distortion of the word
"world" to a limited territorial meaning and the restriction of the
spread of the gospel—apt word, spread—to the surface of the
earth better than the Southern Baptist Convention. This church
has a vast overseas mission which is the pride of the denomination.
Its home mission program includes the planting of Southern
churches in every state in the United States despite a gentleman's
agreement dividing the continental United States between it and
the American Baptist Convention. Its lust to expand laterally is
notorious. Yet this church which believes that it is going "into
all the world" pierces with the gospel none of the strata of social
unrest in that region in which it is the dominant religious force.
Somewhere, somehow this church, and along with it all the other

churches in varying degrees, has mistaken the earth for the world and missionary scope for redemptive thoroughness.

Second, there persists in all of the churches, in some more than others, the medieval belief that the church is a sacred precinct, a "God's house" in the strictest sense. There and there only God lives, and to this sanctuary calls all men out of the world. This mood establishes divisions and oppositions which are entirely contrary to the spirit of the gospel: the church and the world, the temple and the temporality, the secular and the profane. What the churches have not yet seen, are only dimly beginning to see, is that there can be no sanctification of all existence until there has been a secularization of all existence. It was to the world that Christ was sent, not to the church. He was born in a stable, of a maiden and wrapped, as all new-born babies of his day were, in swaddling clothes. As Karl Heim in *The Nature of Protestantism* put the thought most tenderly and persuasively: "Man can serve God only by helping his fellowmen. In every place the world is impure, in the monastery as well as outside of it; and in every place it may be the throne of grace, the nonspacial realm in which the Christ is invisibly present and accessible. His gracious presence is omnipresent and cannot be confined to a eucharistic tabernacle. 'Foxes have holes and birds of the air have nests; but the Son of man has nowhere to lay his head.' Christ wanders homelessly through the centuries. He is nowhere and everywhere."[1]

If this view is part of the nature of Protestantism, Roman Catholicism has learned and practices the lesson of it quite as well as Protestantism. The tragedy is that neither branch of the Christian faith—Protestant, Orthodox or Roman Catholic—has as yet grasped the full significance, the social as well as the personal and cosmic meaning, of that Incarnation in which the Word became flesh and God in unique intrusion entered the world. For the Incarnation broke the wall between time and eternity, temple and market, church and shop, sacred and secular. The Incarnation

[1] Philadelphia, Fortress Press, 1963, p. 137. (German ed., Leipzig, Quelle and Meyer, 1929.)

allows no division of the gospel into personal and social, permits no surrender of the group to the devil in order to rescue one member of it from him, lets no public injustice escape the gospel's judgment while the gospel tends some private man's grief. The God who assumed flesh sought the redemption of the whole man in all his circumstances and conditions. Forgetting this, the church ceases to be the church of the Incarnated Christ.

Third, Christians have defaulted their social duty because they have viewed history as separate national, racial, social, ethnic and biographical strands rather than as one stream of intricate and interrelated world events. This erroneous distinction has enabled the churches to concentrate their energies on some aspects of man's pilgrimage and withhold them entirely from others. Until the 15th century and for some time thereafter human history could be viewed as several separate histories. The American Indians were until then ocean-locked in their hemisphere; the Eskimos were ice-bound in the north; the natives of Central Africa were trapped in jungles and cut off by the Sahara Desert from European and Mediterranean civilization; the Chinese, Indians and Polynesians were tied to the western world only by the romantic reports of daring Marco Polo's. In the 20th century the interdependence of all people is an established and daily demonstrated fact which cannot be disputed and which can be ignored only at great peril to all peoples. The ghettoization of ethnic and racial groups—which may once have served good purposes—now threatens to explode any society which compels it. The division of the individual into his personal, family, social, physical, economic selves, each to be treated according to a specific diagnosis and prescription, is no longer permitted by our modern understanding of the whole man. The isolation of religious man from political and scientific man can be accomplished on paper but not in real life. Human history is a massive glacier which carries everything human with it as it moves, receiving in its bulk all the feeding streams and carrying them away. The church which omits any fleck or fissure of that glacier from the compass of its concerns betrays its Lord and abandons its people.

Fourth, Christians in great masses have viewed man's "salvation" in terms so highly personalized and other-worldly that they cannot ascribe any social significance to the phrase "redemption." No matter how tightly they squeeze the concept, "child of God," with its inclusive connotations, they will not accept the concept "family of God," in its inclusive meanings. So in white churches we get Christians who have no discernible malice toward Negroes but who refuse to participate in social, political or legislative programs to end the segregation of Negroes or to rescue them from oppressing discrimination. They grant that racial prejudice is a sin but see that sin only in its sharply individualistic sense. They grant that racial inequalities defy God's justice as well as man's but are convinced that they can be removed only by a one-by-one conversion of men to brotherly love. They will not grant that collective action of any kind—even legal and peaceful action— is incumbent upon the Christian citizen either as citizen or as Christian. There are many Christians, to be sure, for whom such reasoning is a ruse, a rationalization of their will to keep the Negro segregated and oppressed; but there are nevertheless many Christians conscientiously committed only to those programs of social justice which depend upon the conversion of individual men. For them public actions, collective actions, coercive actions, however nonviolent and however legal, are vulgar and unbecoming to a Christian. Paragons of personal morality individually, such Christians are collectively a block to Christian social action. In every community social ills persist not only because of evil, scheming men but also because of good men who believe sincerely that the collective welfare depends entirely upon the one-by-one conversion of individual men.

Fifth, Christians in several of the churches studied in this volume fail their social duty because they innocently or purposefully confuse the church-state issue with the issues of social Christianity. Tell a congregation of Protestant Christians that Christian ethics summons their support of a specific piece of legislation, and more frequently than not you will receive back the amusing but frustrating *non sequitur:* "We must keep religion out of politics and politics out of religion." When a certain local Protestant church was encouraged to support a municipal survey to determine the scope of racial discrimination in its city, the strongest argument against the participation of the church in the survey was that church and state must be kept separate. The acceptance of Negro members by this church was fought out and resolved several years ago on the sound basis that Christ's family is not divisible by racial distinction; yet church members hesitated to take up the matter of the social oppressions suffered by the Negro members, arguing that political and legislative action violates the separation of church and state principle. Here, too, this apology for social inactivity rises sometimes from an innocent misunderstanding of the First Amendment to the Constitution of the United States and sometimes from a wily resistance to all social change.

There is no agreement on the precise meaning and specific implications of the First Amendment, no consensus among religious people as to how and how far church and state should be separate functions of one people, no universal acceptance of Jefferson's phrase "wall of separation." Whatever the First Amendment means, certainly it was not the intention of the founding fathers —most of whom were religious men—to withhold the wisdom of religion or the devotion and ability of religious men from the government of the nation. Obviously they saw dangers in a state either dominated by or too heavily influenced by a church, and they saw dangers for any church bound to or by the state. It was not their intention to paralyze the governing function of religious men or to relieve them of their social responsibility. They sought to cut off forever the ecclesiastical control of civil government and prevent forever civil infringements of religious freedom. They saw in the First Amendment not the stifling but the release of religious energies for the benefit of a people voluntarily bound together in a healthful way for the fullest and freest exercise of religion. To use the First Amendment as a block to the penetration of government by religion contravenes the intentions of the First Amendment. We are bound together in the United States, as the Preamble to the Constitution states, "to establish justice, insure domestic tranquility, provide for the common defense, promote the general welfare, and secure the blessings of liberty to ourselves and our posterity." Justice, tranquility, defense, welfare and liberty are religious as well as political and social terms. They belong neither to the state nor to the church; they belong to man. They are words which rebuke every form of injustice, inequity, disadvantage and oppression and which summon both government and church to their support. A personal piety which neglects these areas of our common life, however beautiful that piety may be, is civil irresponsibility and religious heresy.

Sixth, rapid social change has moved so fast and so far in this century, and the churches have moved so slowly, that the churches have been left far behind. To say nothing of automation, urbanization, cybernetics, international weaponry—areas of rapid development in which even the nature of change has changed—in the area of race relations the progress of the problem and its solution moves so fast that it is no longer relevant to ask what the church should do for the Negro but, as we shall see, what the racial problem is doing to the churches. In his little book *Race and the Renewal of the Church,* Will D. Campbell said that the church "has waited too long to carry out its mandate, and to a large part of the world, what we Christians do from here on out really does not matter very much."[2] This is not an hysterical judgment. Even now, while the greater part of the church is trying to make up its mind as to whether the racial problem is its problem, the racial struggle passes the church by and goes on down the street.

Somewhere, I think in his Yale lectures, Henry Ward Beecher told the story of a walk through the woods with his dog. Along the way the dog chased a woodchuck into a hollow log and stood

[2] Philadelphia, Westminster, p. 3.

for a time barking at the hidden woodchuck. On every walk after that, said Beecher, when he and the dog came to the hollow log the dog would stop and bark. And that, Beecher told the Yale seminarians, is the church: It barks at hollow logs long after the issue has gone. For many Christians today, many in the churches treated in this volume, the issues are: science versus religion, evolution versus a literalistic biblical account of creation, historical criticism versus an infallible Bible, social salvation versus personal salvation, theological liberalism versus fundamentalism. These battles were fought out and settled years ago, but Christians still bark at the empty logs. The new problems sweep over us and through us—problems of ethnic and racial relationships which tax all human ingenuity, problems of embarrassing abundance and humiliating poverty side by side, of unprofitable leisure and unwanted idleness, of exploding populations, of ignorance, disease, urban decay, crime-ridden cities, increasing mental and emotional instability, adult and juvenile delinquency, broken homes, alcoholism, threatening nuclear holocausts. So run the real problems, passing the churches by; for the churches are otherwise engaged, preoccupied with hollow logs.

Seventh, in part the churches' nerve of social alertness and concern has been deadened, crushed, by the massiveness of the problems. Some of the social issues confronting the churches are so immense, have accumulated so much momentum, that they sweep the church along, battered and insensible, in their undertow. The posture of most of the churches vis-à-vis the threat of thermonuclear war, for example, is more a gesture of helpless despair than an attitude of resolute defiance. The Swiss slogan, "History is governed by human confusion and by divine providence," expresses the biblical view of history in a witty economy of words. The first half of that saying poses no problem for modern man; the second half does, even for Hebraic-Christian man. He is more fatalistic than biblical in his historical view, inclined to surrender the massive issues to whatever fates, if any, control them rather than to a sovereign Creator who knows what he is doing with his creation. Modern man, modern Christian man, knows the reign of human confusion; he is not too sure that beyond this confusion a divine providence governs imperially. And a man who doubts that God governs the titanic sweeps of history is not much disposed to try, either alone or through his church, to remedy, control and direct events which appear even beyond God's power.

Eighth, to a large extent churches in the United States survive as rural remnants in an urban society. The urbanization of the churches lags behind the urbanization of most institutions. Some members of a city church served a decade ago by the author used to call it the largest country church in the big city. They were referring to the friendliness of the communicants. But something more than rural friendliness survives in many metropolitan churches. Too sophisticated to acknowledge that they perpetuate a rural mentality, these churches nevertheless honor and observe an agrarian philosophy which stresses heroic individualistic solutions of personal problems but rejects collective action. Unfortunately the rural terms in which much of the gospel was necessarily first delivered tend to prolong in the churches an agrarian perspective which sees American life in long outmoded patterns.

There is nothing wrong *per se* with an agrarian philosophy in an agrarian setting. But increasingly American society is megapolitan—that is, composed of massive population complexes: Milwaukee to Chicago to Gary, Indiana; Boston to New York to Philadelphia to Washington to Norfolk; Los Angeles and its satellites. The recent United States Supreme Court ruling on redistricting for congressional elections is another proof of what Blake McKelvey in *The Urbanization of America* called "the triumph of metropolitan regionalism." Even if we grant that the basic human problems—man and himself, man and his neighbor, man and God, man and nature—have not changed since Eden and will not change until history's end, we cannot ignore the fact that these problems express themselves one way on the farm and in the village and quite differently in urban and suburban

America. Compared with city man the farmer had few social problems, and what he did have were relatively simple. The social life of metropolitan man, even if he lives alone in a "high-rise" and never speaks to anyone, is vast and intricate. However impersonal and depersonalizing the societal pressures which play upon urban man, they differ in form, degree and intensity from those which rural man experienced. Problems unimaginable in rural America are commonplace in the nation's industrialized, congested megapolises. When the church brings to urban pressures and problems which are new in their size and shape a rural view of the gospel rather than the gospel's view of man in all his settings and relationships, it distorts the gospel and abandons the city.

The platform from which we have to view the coming relationship of the church and man's social, political and economic struggles does not encourage optimism. Except for the racial issue's jabbing of the churches' conscience, there appears little possibility that the churches will come abreast of the times, see their social duty and accept their mission to the world in something more than an evangelistic sense. The crucial question in the coming generation, as I have implied, may be therefore not what the churches do for the world but what a people-crammed, fast-moving, world-in-conflict does to the churches. Is it a sacrilegious paraphrase to say for our day that God so loved the church that he sent the world that the church might not perish? Certainly the world in our time puts "now or never" challenges to the churches. Ignored, those challenges will destroy the churches, letting them remain in their material grandeur but isolating them from man's real life as a living organism walls off and renders inert harmless cysts. On the other hand the pressures, threats and pleas of the world may be the catalysts which revive, reform and activate the churches.

Let us take one illustration, the potentially corrective impact of the racial struggle upon the churches. What is the meaning of the increasing hubbub at the doors of white, Anglo-Protestant

churches as Negroes are turned away by force or slur or are
received in electric silence? There is a difference of opinion, but
Christian perception can see in this strange and painful event a
creative God doing a new thing with the churches. Christian
history teaches that though churches continue through their natural heirs, they are reformed by their adopted children. Churches
have their continuity through the descendants of their own families in a kind of Lois to Eunice to Timothy progression, but
they have their revival through the acceptance of previously rejected neighbors. In the first century a Jewish Christianity, in
danger of becoming an obscure sect, received a powerful renewal
when Paul and his companions took the gospel to the Greeks and
the Romans and Peter, seeing a vision, approved the mission to
the Gentiles. When Rome was falling and the wisest minds of the
time thought that the church was falling with it, the Ostrogoths
and the Visigoths, converted to Jesus Christ, supplied the life
and future of the church.

White Anglo-Protestants have been asking themselves what
can save a decadent Protestantism, freeing it from its middle-class
prison, its suburban slavery, its stifling genteel mentality, its prim
and proper morality, its preoccupation with itself. The answer
is the Gentile, the "other," whomever we do not want and in
boorish or subtle ways reject. For white Protestantism the Gentile
is the Christian Negro, and for Negro Protestantism the Gentile
is the white Christian. What each fears—the disappearance of
white and Negro churches and the emergence of socially, racially,
ethnically inclusive churches—may be the best hope, if not the
last, for reformed, renewed Protestantism.

If it comes, this merger of white and Negro Protestantism will
compel a painful but beneficial restructuring of the center of
Protestant church life. The greatest common denominator of
Protestant church life is its familial character. But when this togetherness transgresses the nature of the church, it produces evil
rather than good. True, the members of any local church should
feel themselves one family, but we have used the wrong kind of

glue to achieve this bond. That is, the familial quality of Protestant church life rests upon personal congeniality, similarity of taste, equality of social status. We are too often a church family not because of what we share in Christ but because of what we share in the world.

The British theologian P. T. Forsyth gave the answer to this problem a long time ago, and we have not yet paid serious attention to what he said. He wrote: "Sacraments, not socialities, make the center of our church life and social unity." Exactly! Almost every collective sin of the churches springs from the fact that they achieve their cohesiveness through socialities. Racial exclusiveness; social snobbery; aloofness from the arenas in which men struggle, toil, sweat and die; antiseptic quarantine from the diseases of the world—these sins are all due to the fact that in local Protestant churches most people love one another for the wrong reason. Our solidarity as Christians does not spring from the fact that we are washed and made acceptable to each other by the same cultural and racial streams but from the fact that we have a common baptism. Our unity as Christians does not rise from our common tastes but from our common Supper. The Christian family must remain, but it must be a *Christian* family. At least the racial problem compels us to ask questions about the nature of Protestant church life. Perhaps in this way the inscrutable God forces us to restructure the center of Protestant life.

It may well be also that the healthiest sound in the white churches today is the angry rumbling of dissatisfaction which sweeps through the churches among the young ministers and laymen, a dissatisfaction with the aloofness of the churches from the plight of the Negro. In loud, sometimes uncouth voices young Christians remind us that Christians are not custodians of a shrine, not imprisoned caretakers of a sacred institution, but were created, gathered, sent as God's consecrated priests to serve him in that great church which is the world.

As does the racial problem, so does every other social issue in its own way drive us toward that Head of the Church who sends his people into the world. For the Christian life occurs in the world—where Christ was crucified—or it does not occur at all. The future of the churches and the future of Christianity may still be inseparably intertwined, but if this is to remain so, the churches must go as messengers and servants into *all* the world.